FROM UNSTOPPABLE *to* UNCOACHABLE

A New Yesterday Tomorrow - A Network Marketing Journey from Stupidville to Failure City (via Disillusion Junction)

by PEGGY PEAK

ISBN 978-1-9196073-0-6 (paperback)
ISBN 978-1-9196073-1-3 (ebook)

Published by IBII in 2021
www.peggypeak.co.uk

CONTENTS

PREFACE

Oh boy, where do I start? For years, I harboured the idea of committing my deathless prose to paper. I promised myself I'd return to writing during the Covid-19 lockdown. After all, there are only so many lockdown jigsaws a person can tolerate before jigsaw-puzzler's cramp twists their arm into the shape of a pretzel. Yet the impulse to autobiography snuck into my conscious mind only this year, 2020, while I explored my memory box during a house move.

What to write about, though? I had enjoyed early writing success, publishing my first short story in a popular teen magazine, You & I, in the mid-nineties. This was around the time the micro-miniclad Spice Girls hit the pop scene like a tsunami, shouting about what they really, really wanted, which, if I remember correctly, was a zigazig-ah!

I was 17 and as naïve as a farm girl stepping off the train at King's Cross Station for the first time, with a vacuous smile and a mind to match. Back then, my pretty head was stuffed so full of dreams and ambitions that common sense could gain no foothold. The world, I thought, was my lobster! How wrong could a young girl be—about my life, of course, not the lobster!

There were hundreds of topics in my head. But, having been recently wounded by my experience with MLM, the topic was fresh on my mind. Some may be as familiar with MLM as a couch potato with his TV remote. But for those yet to be initiated into this dark art, MLM stands for Multi-Level Marketing, aka Network Marketing or Direct Selling. I felt, and still do feel, passionate about it, positively and negatively. Decision made, then. I would write a memoir of my two-year exploration of network marketing. And here it is.

The topics I share are far from trade secrets, so if you're expecting to discover the formula for Pepsi Cola, you'll need to look elsewhere (Search the Internet, you're sure to find someone willing to sell it to you for $10.) Most of the information you'll read here may be found in templates readily available on the Internet or the company's website. However, I won't disclose the company I promoted because that isn't important.

I will disclose that by the time I quit MLM, I had done for the advancement of womankind, what Calamity Jane did for bog-snorkelling—absolutely nothing. The path paved with stars I'd imagined as a young woman; the one that glittered from the primary school gate to a stellar future, contrasted sharply with the actual script of my life: school, job, marriage, mortgaging myself into the 5th dimension, having kids (and those are the highlights!)

And just for the record, I have a loving husband of almost 20 years and two incredible children. Even though my daily routine is as much a nine-to-five grind as the next person's, I have a great job working for a reputable company, so I did not do too badly by following the crowd.

You'll find nothing in this book I didn't experience but had I known that the journey would turn out to be harder than doggie-paddling across a crocodile-infested swamp with my legs tied together, I might never have set off. Yet, I am far from gloomy. On the contrary, I fully intend to re-inflate the inner tube of my ambition, with the bicycle pump of desire, to give my dreams the kiss of life (how's that for a mixed metaphor?) My current goal is to spend the next 25 years of my life radiating more joie de vivre than a Can-Can dancer on opening night!—despite (or perhaps, because of) my MLM trials and tribulations.

I changed some names to protect people's privacy. Also, you should not expect dialogues recorded here to comprise verbatim transcripts. All conversations do, however, convey the essence of what it felt like at the time. I have done as much as anyone could to recall and interpret critical events accurately. Still, this remains a collection of personal impressions from an important episode in my life.

In unfolding my tale, I have tried not to preach. Nor will you get a sales pitch from me. I've tried to confine myself to personal experiences and opinions. Hopefully, along the way, I won't bore you with selfish nostalgia. However, I hope my MLM experience resonates with many, inside and outside the MLM bubble, because its life lessons are universal.

Finally, I hope that you find my account both informative and entertaining. If it is, I'll have done what I set out to do.

Chapter 1

'WHO WANTS TO BE A MILLIONAIRE? I DO!'

In which Peggy contemplates bungee-jumping in the buff— Flirts with Avon, Herbalife, Cable TV, Oriflame, Ann Summers and Kleeneze—And as a result, wonders whether a career in night-shift shelf-stacking at a Lidl's store might afford a brighter future.

Horses for Courses

Like naked bungee jumping off the edge of the Grand Canyon after drinking a bottle of Pinot Grigio, network marketing isn't for everyone. But it is an excellent opportunity for some. Recruiters will make it sound easy, yet stop and think. When you apply for a job in a company with 3,000 employees, how many are destined to earn top dollar? How many shin themselves to the top of the greasy pole and sit there chewing on a fat Havana cigar? Hard to say, but not everybody is born to be Jeff Bezos or Oprah Winfrey, however hard they try.

As I write, in 2020, the whole world is in lockdown, leaving MLM distributors two clear courses of action. They can be as compassionate and understanding as a TV evangelist or bulldoze through sales, recruiting like crazy, targeting the vulnerable who have lost their jobs or have been furloughed. They seem to think this is the right time to brag about their work-from-home opportunity and argue forcefully about the need for Plan B, aka their side hustle.

Sigh

From Hero to Zero in 87 tortuous steps

My simple aim is to share the experience of my failed MLM journey. In doing so, I promise not to preach to you, like a Bible Belt pastor—I have no Good Book to thump here. Nor am I a recruiting sergeant for MLM. Absolutely not. I remain neutral on the issue. Whether you wish to become involved in MLM will always be a matter for you alone. Either way, I wish you luck and good fortune. This isn't an angry book; at least, I never intended it to be.

But just in case I slip, this is my guarantee: In the event of any reader detecting the hint of an anti-MLM snarl in these pages, my solicitor is legally bound to strap me into a medieval ducking stool. Then submerge me in the Manchester Ship Canal until I wise up.

Okay, I'm glad that's out of the way. Now here's an FAQ: Is MLM a—pause for Jaws' shark theme—Pyramid Selling? And here, in MLM-speak, is the standard answer recruits like me trained to trot out: 'You mean like a traditional business? Where the CEO gets paid most money, whilst his direct reports and the minions reporting to them earn the basic wage?'

Another way to reply to this common FAQ is by pretending you just got off the train from Stupidville: 'A pyramid scheme, you say? Aren't they illegal? I would never be part of anything illegal.'

I can honestly say that the Network Marketing company I worked for wasn't that cynical. There was a genuinely good chance you could do well for yourself, even out-earning the person who first introduced you to the business (Take that, Mr Recruiter!)—If you put the work into it.

So, what do I know, where have I been, what have I seen, what is my experience of MLM? As I ponder these questions, I realise that I had quite a bit of exposure over the years. I did not appreciate this at the time, but once I started thinking about my previous exposure to MLM, I realised I knew more than I thought. Like hapless Victorian natural scientists struggling to classify the platypus duck, I still find it difficult to precisely identify MLM businesses unless they sell obvious products like shakes, supplements, or beauty products. But every day's a school day, and I get better at this as we go along.

Cable TV

I was a typical high school student—young, ambitious, keen to raise my disposable income from the level of a sharecropper to that of a Universal Benefit recipient. Recruiting agents tried to enlist students to trudge from door to door hellbent on selling cable TV to the great unwashed. I hesitated no longer than had I been fleeing a burning building, immediately signing up with my best friend (I had never heard of due diligence back then!)

It was a long time ago, but I think we just signed up punters to cable TV direct selling. We didn't hunt in packs like wolves, but we did work in pairs. Once, we got through the front door of this 12-floor apartment building (You shouldn't think Mission Impossible here, we just waited until a legitimate tenant opened the security door and followed them in.) We knocked on every door from the ground floor to the roof with the enthusiasm of kindergarten children on an Easter egg hunt. It wasn't an unpleasant experience.

Cable TV was the greatest thing since sliced bread, and we got many signatures. Not once did we have to wrestle anyone to the ground and incentivise them with a Chinese burn. This is surprising since the channels on offer back then were dire—home shopping feeds running infomercials that took two hours to sell you a Delia Smith endorsed egg poacher. Plus, a 24-hour movie channel stocked with black and white B films, popular with insomniacs desperate to catch forty winks.

Despite the rock bottom quality of the product, we did well. I can't remember how much we earned, but knowing how we were back then, we'd have spent it faster than we made it.

Could you class the selling of Cable TV as MLM? Honestly? I don't know. It was direct selling, however, and that sounded perilously close to MLM.

Avon

Avon is a brand that has been around forever. Or so it seems. Did cavewomen pretty themselves up with Avon products for their favourite cavemen back before the invention of the wheel? I'm basing my theory on how good Wilma and Betty look in the Flintstones but suffice to say that Avon is a brand that has stood the test of time.

My friends back then were, compared to now, rigidly gender-aligned. I had girly girlfriends, boyish girlfriends, girly boyfriends and alpha-male boyfriends. The girly girlfriend gang enjoyed buying Avon mascaras and eye shadows. I had a group all to myself—the not-so-girly-girls. No Avon for me, thank you very much.

Please note that in parts of the British Isles, the selling of Avon is considered a crime. As in the gratuitous Scottish insult, 'Yer Da sells Avon roon the doors!' (Translation: 'Your father retails women's make-up around the estate.')

I could never see why anyone might buy anything from a catalogue. Not when you can get what you want from the shops, thereby avoiding the daily scanning of your cul-de-sac, east and west, for a glimpse of the postman. Some argued that there were plenty of samples to try before you buy. The catch is, who's to know the foundation cream samples weren't high-value, eighty quid a fluid ounce creations, but what got shipped to you would be lawnmower grease in pretty, vanishingly small bottles. In any event, I set the bar low in my make-up standards and consistently failed to get over it.

Another reason the pay-now-place-your-faith-in-the-Royal-Mail method fails to cut it for me is that I am impatient. I never put ketchup on my burger because it takes far too long to get out of the bottle (Come on, Heinz, pull up your socks!)

Herbalife

I only discovered what Herbalife was, 20 years after encountering it, when I got involved with my MLM company; if Cable TV was the best thing since the invention of the under-wire bra, then I suppose Herbalife might have been the next best thing to that.

Herbalife was the talk of the town, but I mustn't have been listening because I knew very little about it—I thought they sold herbs door to door like gipsies of old. When you don't need to drink shakes because regular food works just fine for you, it's a fad not worth fadding about with (Editor note: Is fadding even a verb?)

CDs

What else, oh yes! Direct CD sales. I'm pretty sure this was MLM! I still awake at 3 AM some mornings, shouting, 'It wasn't me, your honour! I wasn't out that night.' Direct selling CDs to innocent citizens may sound benign, but trust me, there were battles in the Crimean war that were less brutal.

I fell into the trap when I replied to an ad 'to earn extra cash'. A charming distributor invited me to accompany her as she plied her trade. We drove out of the city to a small town, parked up in the nearest supermarket, got out of the car with a box of CDs, and plonked ourselves by the front door. We greeted innocent shoppers with a cheerful grin (Grinning is a skill well worth practising in the world of MLM. Just don't overdo it, or you'll get 'grinner's cramp'.)

Before I knew it, I heard the distributor shout 'Congratulations!' to a potential customer. 'You are our one-hundredth customer,' she announced in an exalted tone more applicable to winning a Rolls Royce Silver Shadow for a one-pound raffle ticket than a lowly CD. 'That qualifies you for a discounted price on this CD!'

My face shaded crimson with shame. Those poor people travelled from surrounding villages in pursuit of their weekly shop. Suddenly Lady Luck is kissing their butts. Awesome! I actually can't believe that they bought this lie. They paid top dosh for a cover band's re-mixed version of Chirpy Chirpy Cheep Cheep. They were naïve village people who got fooled easily back in the nineties.

I immediately understood what my apprenticeship was about. I was exhausted from working harder than a Blackpool donkey on a double shift, stacking supermarket shelves all night to pay the bills. Like a News of the World undercover reporter clambering out a window to escape participation in an orgy, I made my excuses and left. Then headed back to the car for some shut-eye.

By the time the sales push came to an end, the distributor had worn her professional grin, chuffed to bits with her day's earnings. 'Would you like to join us?' She asked as we drove back to base.

'Errm, no, thank you, I think shelf-stacking might be the career path for me,' I said.

Sigh

Kleeneze

The Kleeneze catalogue regularly arrived on my doorstep, beamed down, no doubt, by an alien civilisation. I carried it out to the bins holding my nose and brandishing a forked stick the first few times.

When it started arriving with a note that said, 'Please leave me on the step if you don't want to buy anything,' I began to suspect that the catalogue was of terrestrial origin, the note penned by a human and not a Xenomorph.

Not that it made much difference to me. For reasons already stated, I hate catalogues, so I began fishing them out of my letterbox and immediately tossing them on my doorstep.

Oriflame

I have heard of Oriflame - I always thought they sold hoity-toity branded make-up, but yet again, why would I spend the cost of a weekend at a top spa for a small glass jar of wrinkle-blasting gloop out of a glossy periodical?

Ann Summers

And finally, Ann Summers! Did you know this was MLM? Well, I didn't, but it is evident now that I'm a wiser FNM (failed network marketer). I got invited to an Ann Summers party by one of the mums from nursery whose child was friends with my child.

We did not even know each other that well, so I suspect I was there to help reach the mandatory minimum party numbers for a home visit party. Anyway, I enjoyed the party, in the same way I'd appreciate a sauna while wearing a fur coat. It was awkward as hell! I felt compelled to buy something, and let's put it this way: it is still in its wrapper, buried at the bottom of my bedside drawer. And before you ask, it wasn't battery powered!

It wasn't me, your honour!
I wasn't out that night.

Chapter 2

JOURNEY OF A THOUSAND MILES

In which Peggy gets unsolicited advice from a clairvoyant, who foretells a career in MLM — Peggy contemplates being swept from the mundane world of 9-5 to the Land of Milk, Honey and her brand products — Discovers that the step before a dazzling entrepreneurial future involves more than getting others to eat meal replacement products, she is obliged to replace her meals with them too — Brainwashes herself into believing stuff (excludes Jack Frost, the tooth fairy and Santa Claus) that as an adult, she shouldn't!

How did I get introduced to MLM in my forties?

You won't believe me, but I'll tell you anyway. A Clairvoyant introduced me. No, she did not have a crystal ball, it had long been consigned to the cupboard under the stairs, and again no, she didn't gasp, wide-eyed over the tarot cards. But it would be rather funny if she'd been reading my horoscope! 'Ah! Yes, I see now. The moon is in the seventh house, and Jupiter aligns with Mars, and peace will rule the planets' Hold on, that is a song, isn't it? Well, you know what I mean. At no point did she say my future lay in high protein shakes.

Anna

In reality, the clairvoyant and I were just chitchatting before my session. I was telling her about my life, what I aspired to, what my dreams were and about life in general. I wasn't there for her to predict my future. Otherwise, I wouldn't have told her my life story.

Anyway, I told her about my entrepreneurial ambitions to have a private label product and how I had procrastinated for a couple of years before deciding to go for it. When I finally made a move, I realised that I failed to pick the right product.

I launched at the wrong time, with no factual market data analysis behind it. Maybe I thought my product would somehow magic its way to the top of the best sellers' list. There was no demand for the product (two years too late!), and the niche was oversaturated. All this because I was desperate to hop on the side-hustle band waggon, thinking this will turn into the best thing since M&Ms hit the High Street. By the time my corporate contract came to an end, I could entirely focus on my brand-selling and become a millionaire—what the heck, multi-millionaire, let's aim high.

You may well laugh! It never panned out the way I planned. Not surprising since I appeared to have the entrepreneurial flair of a bankrupt. Note to self: Next time you think about pulling a stunt like this, have some start-up capital tucked away in your handbag. Oh, and maybe some reserves for inventory re-order. Duh!

Now, where was I? Oh yes. So there I was, with my lovely, lovely clairvoyant Anna. Me whining like a brat when she said, 'Have you considered selling somebody else's product?'

'Well, of course,' I replied, 'but I have scruples—I want to sell something ethical, something I truly believe in, something that makes an impact in people's lives. Something I would be proud to put my name to.'

I went on—there was no stopping me. 'I know lots of people who've made a small fortune by ordering a tonne of bamboo chopsticks from Shanghai for 3 Yuan, printing a fake Zen Kōan on each (what is the sound of one chopstick clicking?) and selling them singly as 12th-century meditation aids, for ten quid a piece on Amazon. But I have morals, and I cannot bring myself to do stuff like that.'

My lovely, lovely clairvoyant, Anna, said: 'That's perhaps why you are still an employee, grinding out a 9-5, waiting for success to jump up on your lap like a house cat and lie on its back, purring.' Immediately, I mentally downgraded Anna from the lovely, lovely Anna to just the lovely Anna—for rattling the bars of my complacency. It didn't stop her from telling it like it was, though.

'Companies are selling exactly what you are looking for, with no upfront cost or inventory,' said Anna. And BOOM! Just like that, she introduced me to a health and wellness company and a cosmetics company. Smooth! No hard-selling! She just dropped it into the conversation like a seasoned spy (The name's Bond, Anna Bond, licenced to recruit pyramid sellers). She knew her stuff.

Her upline would have been so proud! She said she had two friends who worked for one of the companies, and she was happy to introduce me. I could even choose between health and wellness or cosmetics. What a deal!

I went home that night with thoughts crashing around my head like steel balls in a pinball machine. I tried to be practical. I was no oil painting. I didn't have a Hollywood skin routine. I didn't own or use many cosmetics. I'd practically wash and go, draw on the end of my eyebrows, apply a bit of mascara, and voila! Job done. Was there any reason I couldn't fulfil my wildest cosmetics dreams while doing the weekly shop in Tesco? Remember, I am low maintenance when it comes to beauty products.

On the other hand, I felt a tad porky, you might say. I dreamed one night that my doctor told me that if I put on ten more pounds, I'd have my own gravitational field! The truth is that although I am health conscious, generally eat well and regularly exercise, my weight started to creep up. So I decided to give the health and wellness company a whirl.

The lovely, lovely Anna (I upgraded her again after my mini-tantrum) started a three-way messenger group chat. She introduced me to Simone, who knew everything I needed to know.

Simone

Simone arranged to call me the following day at 6 PM, but I was running late, so I messaged her to ring me half an hour later when I got home because I didn't want to take the call from the car. Once I got home, I ran upstairs with pen and paper and sprang onto the bed like a mountain goat when the phone rang. It was Simone. But she wasn't alone. She'd brought her partner, Carl.

Odd. Was this an episode of the Twilight Zone? They took turns explaining stuff and asking questions. Yet, I was still none the wiser as to what health and wellness meant in their company. I wanted to know what they expected me to do. What would I sell? How would I sell it? It made no sense at all. Remember, I didn't understand Network Marketing, despite my earlier, brief and unwitting exposure to it. I had no idea how it worked. I just thought somebody was selling me something overpriced from a catalogue. I was clueless about getting customers, then distributors, whilst purchasing and using the products myself. I was as confused as a man placed in a barrel and told to pee in the corner. My confusion surfaced in my questions.

'And I need to get my husband signed up, as well as my sister-in-law, her butcher and his next-door neighbour?' What!? OMG, I wasn't prepared to share all this with my husband yet. Geez!

This whole concept was so alien to me. I do not think I understood it, even superficially, at least for the first few months. A quarter of a century later, I'm still naïve.

Stop the world; I want to get off!

'Do you have all the information you need to sign up today, Peggy?'

I became a tad suspicious. My inner Agatha Christie had arisen from her slumber. And I'd watched enough episodes of Murder She Wrote to spot a deception when I saw one.

'Huh? Wait, what? I don't even know how to spell the name of the company!'

I'm sorry, but I don't print money. And you'd have to be the kind of fool who'd buy the London Eye for a fiver from a bloke in a £30 suit and a pair of car-boot-sale trainers, to part with five hundred pounds over the phone, to a stranger, however much they sounded like a favourite relative. Besides, why am I talking to two people?

When I asked her to spell the company's name so that I could Google it (an absolute crime that puts you on a par with Hannibal Lecter in the MLM distributor's mind), she said she would email me some *useful* information on the company. 'Useful for whom?' Piped up my inner Agatha. They said they would send me the good stuff—founder information and other trivia—because, as she put it, Google was awash with people nastier than the child catcher from Chitty Chitty Bang Bang. Many hellbent on besmirching the company's good name by calling them scammers.

Agatha doesn't buy it, so why should I?

Neither Agatha nor I bought this line. 'But, Anna said I wouldn't have any upfront cost?'

'Think if of a reallocation of your monthly grocery shopping budget,' they said cheerily. Were they bonkers? I'm not the sort of consumer who spends five hundred quid on shopping just for myself? I wouldn't pay five hundred quid for a summer holiday in Alicante. I fed my husband, two kids, a dog and a rabbit for a month on that budget.

I ended up bewildered. The buzz words, the relentless positivity, far from enthusing me, were causing me to feel as if I'd misplaced a winning lottery ticket. Just when I felt as if I should end it all by throwing myself off Beachy Head with a small fire safe tucked down the back of my Pretty Polly tights, they started, at last, to explain what I had to do.

High expectations

It turns out they expected me to drink meal replacement shakes. These were so jam-packed full of nutrients that I wondered how they got them all into the bottle. Most of these nutrients originated in the rain forests of Guatemala.

'One meal costs no more than a coffee,' they said as if this was a fact worth ringing the chapel bell for and telling all the villagers.

Wow! I knew coffee formed a regular part of people's lives, but not mine. I didn't trek across town every morning for a Mocha Chocolata, ya-ya and an overpriced muffin! Do you? I make my own breakfast and lunch, and I certainly do not spend eight to ten pounds daily on myself. I will talk about objections in further chapters, but this was always something I could not justify because Shirley Bassey's *Hey big spender* definitely didn't have me in mind. I lived well above the poverty line, and I received no State benefits, but I certainly didn't dine out for breakfast and lunch or get take-aways

As promised, Simone sent over a ton of information. The rebel in me just went right ahead and Googled the company and all the info in Simone's email to validate everything. Any bare-faced lies and they could go whistle for my five hundred quid.

Given time to take in and process Simone's info in my own time to evaluate the pros and cons of the Network Marketing game, I eventually decided to give it a go. The biz sounded super easy, mainly since the product sold itself. Besides, I could afford to lose some weight. Decision made then.

Bowls of nutritious steam!

'You there, take my credit card! And you here's our hard-earned £800 for me and my husband's order. The kids? Don't worry your pretty little head about them, Simone, we'll feed them bowls of steam until we turn a profit.' Good job. I had already finished my Christmas shopping. In 3 months, I could be rolling in it, so I needed to make sacrifices.

I made the order in the middle of December, intending to start on 1st January. How convenient! Diet either begins on Monday or 1st January. We were both as excited as squirrels in a monkey nut factory. We cunningly decided to pig out on extra food until midnight on New Year's Eve to fatten up a bit more. The aim is to dazzle everyone by how well these products worked when we shed all our excess weight. All our friends would be super-psyched, coming down in their droves with sign-up fever. It would rain credit card details, and we'd move to millionaires' row! Hooray!

Did I understand MLM?

No. But I pretended I did! (Palm slaps my forehead with force.)

What I did not realise this early in my MLM journey was that the 3-way call was scripted. Simone and Carl did a fantastic job ensuring the script was natural as possible, but it all sounded as vague as a politician's promise. Suddenly—wallop! Out of nowhere, they want you to order.

I thought we were just chatting and getting to know each other, but these were well-polished sales tactics I'd not come across yet. I usually put the phone down on anybody trying to sell me anything over the phone, like time-share apartments in Beirut (free armed guard for the first three buyers!) That's not strictly true about hanging up because, strictly speaking, I don't even pick up phone calls from unknown callers. I already have double, triple and quadruple glazing, cavity wall insulation, and I'm not expecting a rebate from HMRC.

Anyway, I signed up.

Since I'd signed up voluntarily, I had no one now to blame but myself. Yet the voices whispering in my head used words like 'scam', 'pyramid scheme,' and 'What have you done this time, girl?'

But I have many times been invited onto Private Facebook pages and many other social media groups where I witnessed video footage of the fantastic results achieved by shiny, happy people. They held up their products in front of their newly installed luxury saunas or recently purchased Arabian stallion. These people had what I wanted—everything they'd ever need.

I see now that I had brainwashed myself into believing this was the opportunity of a lifetime—my one in a million shot at stardom. I was going to make it like the elite distributors of the company. The compensation plan was so generous; they were practically giving you money. You order, get two friends to order and boom! You get yourself a good bonus, and your order is virtually paid for. Easy peasy!

Before you start up an unmerited round of applause for my benefit, I should confess that I had not realised the rules of this scheme were more complicated than the assembly instructions for a B&Q chest of drawers.

I can't tell you what I'm selling; want to buy some anyway?

What I failed to realise at the time was that success loves speed. I decided to employ a time-proven sales technique mastered by losers the world over. Its technical name is 'not telling anybody you have anything to sell.'

I had the planet's best nutrition in my kitchen, waiting for New Year's Day to be opened and sampled. I wanted to try the products first. How could I recommend a product I had not tried myself?

But results take time. And time is the enemy of the direct seller. You can lounge about on a fluffy cloud, twanging your harp and not selling for the rest of eternity once you get to heaven. Until then, better get your selling pants on, sister, 'cause time's a-wastin'.

Time is running out on you from the second you sign up, not when you gulp down your first shake. All the best promotions and extra bonuses happen within a tight timeframe. I missed out because I didn't understand the compensation plan, nor was I willing to share the product until I was comfortable with it. I had to be the product of the product. If I looked like a supermodel at forty, everybody would want to join, wouldn't they?

I knew I had to make more friends, start chatting to whoever crossed my path. Not quite the winos on the town hall steps, but pretty much everyone else. I had to add them to my friends list, start posting encrypted posts on my FB wall with tons of emojis, all in public mode (!!), and preach.

They call them 'create curiosity' posts. I call them bloody annoying posts. Do you know the irritating itch that suddenly springs up out of nowhere, ingenuously situated under your shoulder blade where no hand can quite reach? Well, curiosity posts are more annoying than those.

You are instructed to start selling to all your friends. Oops, did I say that out loud? I mean sharing, not selling. That made me feel like I'd recently eaten a dodgy shrimp. We all use social media for different purposes, I know. I like to chat with my friends, posting comments and jokes here and there, just generally keeping in touch through likes and chitchats because we all live in different parts of the world.

I'd post the occasional motivational quote, too ('You can pick your friends and you can pick your nose, but you can't pick your friend's nose'). Still, I used social media to tell people I didn't see very often about the places I visited, the food I made or ate. I am one of those people who post HD photographs of their Toad-in-the-Hole on their FB wall—well, nobody said we have to be friends, or if my kids said something funny or inappropriate.

Axe Grinder Atkinson et al.

All this was in a safe circle of friends. I rejected anyone I did not know on my Facebook. Especially men with hand tools in their names: Angle Grinder Atkinson, Pickaxe Patterson, and anyone else that sounded like they'd get regular invitations to the Wormwood Scrubs Christmas Party. After all, it's meant to be a 'friends list', not yellow pages, right? Wrong! Not if you're serious about making it as a network marketer.

I immediately regretted having 'tidied up' my friends list two years prior. I had close to 200 people listed. There is no way I knew that many people personally, so I reduced it to the realistic 120 or so people I honestly interacted with or whose journeys I found interesting. Now that I needed to extend my audience again, I slowly started to request those 'defriends' back. I just clicked 'Add Friend' without any explanation, acting as if they'd dropped off my list by accident.

Cringe

Suddenly my newsfeed flooded with *appropriate* content and Ads for MLM, and suddenly I started to notice people that worked for other MLM companies. 'Oh, these pills do wonder for your nails and hair; look at my glowing skin. They are the best. PM me if you want to try.' I had been MLM blind in the past. Or maybe I did not pay attention? Admittedly, there are way too many funny animal videos to watch on your feed, especially cats doing stupid stuff like making prank calls (I think these are fake).

I learned early that many MLM companies are American and that different cultures perceive MLM differently. The scripts, the jargon and the materials were full-on 'American', stuff you couldn't pull on a Brit unless you pray on naïve, young, or desperate souls. And I never had the stomach for that.

Of course, your upline (the person who signed you up) will say it's 'stepping outside your comfort zone', but to me, it was just ruthless behaviour. 'But they deserve to know, Peggy. You must share it with everybody; you don't know if they need the extra cash; you can't deny them this opportunity. Let them decide for themselves.' I was labelled selfish for not letting the world and his wife know (Yeah, right!)

There's gold in them thar hills! Really?

Abso-bloody-lutely. You wouldn't exactly trip over six-figure income earners and millionaires, but they are there in every company. Some outstanding leaders work their socks off and, to my mind, deserve every penny. But there are also ruthless Wolf of Wall Street type distributors who are pushy, salesy, and will kick dead bodies to one side to achieve millionaire status.

Did I strike the mother lode?

Abso-bloody-lutely not!

I was prepared to accept that any journey of a thousand miles starts with a single step, but nobody told me that every single one of those steps was going to be uphill!

Chapter 3

NOTHING SUCKS SEEDS LIKE A BUDGERIGAR (EXCEPT SUCCESS)

In which Peggy contemplates setting out on an expedition to locate Eldorado, the Lost City of Gold — instead discovers something far more elusive, a company with morals, ethics and family values — Peggy discovers that her brief is to keep the wool pulled over her customers' eyes — Enters a world in which 'No' means 'Not yet!' — tries on the title 'Lady Shake' for size — ponders secret millionaire status.

All in the family—the dynamic duo

What I discovered about the founders of this fantastic US company gave me goosebumps. It gave my goosebumps goosebumps. Theirs was a real family business. By 'family', I don't mean that they behaved like a branch of the Costa Nostra; more like the Osmonds or the Waltons—close-knit and mutually supportive (although that could describe the mafia too!)

Anyway, the brace of human dynamos leading the charge comprised an experienced, retired couple of MLM professionals. Despite their age, they were the entrepreneurial equivalent of Saturn V rocket boosters. They joined forces with the man who created the world-class products I would sell, my bad again; I meant share. The creator of the product claimed that the use of these products saved his life. How's that for an endorsement!?

This incredible team displayed the passion of an opera singer. They burned to share their enthusiasm with the world and his wife (her butcher and his next-door neighbour.) The company had been running successfully for over 15 years, unshackled by debt. When mapped on paper, the current growth trajectory shot upwards exponentially, like a £10 rocket. These products had positively impacted millions of people's lives, and the rush was on to expand into other global markets (pauses for breath!)

Ring the mission bells!

Their mission statement and core values impressed me. We banged the same drum with equal enthusiasm. Here, finally, was a product to which I could put my name. For this cause, I was thrilled to put my shoulder to the grindstone and my nose to the wheel, put my best foot forward, and reach for the stars. Anatomically, that's almost impossible to do, but I was willing to try.

Anna was dead right. This company's values included integrity, purpose, family, freedom. They were ethically and environmentally aware that if someone set fire to a car tyre in Chipping Sodbury, they could smell it in Leeds. They would arrange for Greenpeace to bulldoze the eco offender's house into the ground within the hour. They were also innovative enough to review ways to reduce their carbon footprint constantly.

They wanted all their distributors—associates they called them—to mirror their core values, treat everyone with respect, never over-promise or exaggerate results, whether financial or physical. It's hard to believe, but they wanted to put the truth where Mildew and Scullery from the X-files always said it was: out there!

I want to make an important point here. So grab a cup of your favourite brew, sit down and listen up. Gordon Greed and his close partner Johnny Ignorance stalk the corridors of every business, from soup kitchens to the boardrooms of crypto-traders, regardless of whether that business is corporate or MLM. It's human nature. The lure of the greenback (Anyone for easy money? Jump aboard, I'm heading that way myself! It's just around the next corner.) Yet I swear that the founders of this company demanded honesty, at all times, from their associates. We were always to do 'the right thing.'

To a man and woman, the corporate team displayed a seemingly unbounded and youthful enthusiasm for their calling, regardless of their age. I heard only praise for them. 'The customer is King' was the motto by which they lived. OMG, they were available—by phone or email—and that's quite something nowadays, when many websites bury their contact numbers in the darkest corners of their websites, hoping they'll be as easy to find as truffles.

In practice, I rarely used their services because the information I needed constantly rained down around me like ticker-tape at a Fourth of July parade. I had no time to question anything. I had answers, articles and posts at my fingertips on a thousand relevant subjects.

Going beyond where no man has gone behind before

There was a time when cockiness overcame me (I'm human too, you know!) I reached out to corporate people in South America, Europe and Asia. Although I haven't counted them personally, there are billions of people on this planet, and I thought I'd tap into their markets too.

None of my English friends showed interest. They looked at me in the same way they might look at a mute Elvis Presley impersonator on stage at an amateur talent night. I exhausted my list and started 'cold calling'. All global corporate offices promptly answered email requests for documentation and templates—a big shout out to all Head Offices.

They organised training for all the associates, set up Zoom meetings, lobbied leaders to speak to us wannabe millionaires, prepared templates, and organised significant annual events. They worked hard and smiled all the time. Like all associates, I had my customisable website, using easily rearrangeable drag-and-drop templates. Very convenient.

Stop the bus!

To help us sell more effectively, the company provided every kind of high-tech, state-of-the-art doohickey. The quality of which would make a computer geek dance the sailor's hornpipe with glee. Yet, associates knew from the outset that it wasn't the done thing to advertise the company on our social media outlets because the URL link would give away the company's name!

Say, what?!

There was a stunt as challenging to pull off, as tightrope walking across Niagara Falls on a washing line using a cocktail stick with a cherry skewered on both ends for balance. Running a business without telling customers what I did, nor what it was I was promoting?

I felt like a mugger, lurking in the dark, opportunistically waiting for passing victims. Or closer to the truth, waiting for somebody to comment or 'like' my 'mysterious' post—the one intended to pique the curiosity of the unaware punter, before dropping a message on them that hopefully sparked a conversation—'Come into my parlour,' said the spider to the fly!

From there, we were but a hop, skip and a jump away from the pincer manoeuvre of the three-way call, during which my upline and I would attempt to kettle the prospect into a corner and—what?—get them to feel the way I felt: deeply uncomfortable? ('American Express? Barclaycard? A bank draft from your terminally ill granny? Any of those will do nicely. If you'd rather do cash, I can supply you with a small hammer with which to burst your children's piggy banks asunder. That'll be five hundred quid, s'il vous plaît.')

I knew many successful people who branded themselves by building their own websites. They were rich and as sophisticated as a Walnut Whip. Sod it; I will do that, I decided. I purchased a domain name and the *.co.uk* and *.com* to go with it.

Unfortunately, as it turned out, I left both domains hanging in the breeze like two damp socks on a washing line. You see, there was a sparring match going on in my head—my very own Rumble in the Jungle. In the red corner, my integrity; in the blue corner, cold, hard dosh.

Was I ready to be known as 'Lady Shake?' Would I go by the title 'Shake-ira?' That would be a legacy I might end up trying to live down in the Colombian market! My original, and dare I say, the humble intention was to make more money than a Mexican drug cartel. Most of it crowding into my offshore account while I lay sleeping if that's okay with you. With that sort of passive income, I would be able to buy inventory of the following whizz-bang product to hit the market. Then I wouldn't have to limit myself to the sole role of MLM professional.

Some millionaire leaders had a different kind of website. These were for training their downline in exactly how to perform their business. They shared this training on YouTube or shared Facebook groups not directly linked to their organisation. But I always suspected they had a secret, invitation-only page for a chosen few, accessible only by keying ALT-CTL-SHIFT-FUNCTION 6 with the screen cam turned on (Don't waste your time trying, I made that one up!)

I don't rightly know. I never got anywhere close to the pros. I was part of a team of strugglers—the going-under-for-the-third time squad of wannabe leaders. They failed to inspire me; I never felt I could emulate their behaviour because what they did seemed desperate, and 'desperate' just wasn't me at all.

What will success look like?

What I'm about to say will sound a bit Zen, but there's only one way to make it in MLM. And that is to be who you are, daddio. To be authentic, man. I'm a private person, uneasy talking to strangers. Of the many things I am not, one of the biggies is an ice-breaker. Let me spell it out—I do not break the ice. That would have to be your job if you wanted to relate to me. Once you break the ice, you'll find me charming and approachable; until then, forget about it!

The funny thing is, when you go to events and hear other people's stories, they all say things like 'I was like you. Private. Shy. I didn't know how to talk to people. Once you realise it is not about you, it's about this gift that somebody shared with you, how would you feel if they never talked to you? You must tell as many people as you can about this gift.'

'Gee thanks,' I'd say (inwardly, of course), 'that's quite a trick you pulled off there, making me feel guilty and crap about myself at the same time. Are you a member of the Magic Circle?'

Since when did 'No' mean 'not now'?

Initially, they expected us to connect with at least ten people a day. You could utilise social media. Facebook, Instagram, LinkedIn—which platform didn't matter. Then you needed to add new people to your list constantly. You could message, text, ring, email, like, share, tweet, swap endearments using semaphore flags, just so long as you communicated. If they say no, that was fine. You just had to remind yourself that no means 'not now', that you could follow up later. Now might not be the right time. They reckoned it took an average of seven follow-ups before somebody finally signed up.

Now let me get this straight: My dictionary is definite on this point—No means bloody NO! Simply asking me to poke people more than twice in the chest about this causes steam to blast from my ears as though from a train whistle.

But what do I know? Maybe I'm 'not coachable' (one of their jargon terms). If so, I had better close down my offshore account. I should have given the system a chance. I should have followed up, remained bosom-buddies with my contacts, until the lucky seventh time of asking when they'd bite my arm off for a chance to grab a piece of the hottest action in town.

Funky Tools and Apps

The UK team had privileged access to a revolutionary MLM app. It didn't wash and iron laundry, make cotton candy or straighten flared trousers, but it did most other things. I could sync contacts, send videos, keep track of my team, manage my social media, get social-media-ready pictures, templates, notifications of payments and various kinds of all-singing, all-dancing stuff.

Seven quid a month. That's all it cost. Some people spend more on cotton buds. No problem if you're earning good money. But I wasn't. So this was just another unwanted expense.

On red-letter days, when I managed to earn some dosh, the company sent the remittance to a different app or a separate app account, which also incurred a monthly account fee. It remains debatable whether I was benefitting, but the banks sure were enjoying my limited success.

The app would make my selling life easier; they claimed, because you had a whole toolbox at your disposal. Somebody asks you a product question; you shoot over an explanatory video. If you don't know what to say to somebody or how to connect with them, you'll find a text message template. It's all there. All you have to do is tweak it to make it more personal, copy and paste, and hit send.

Classify your contacts as 'warm' or 'cold'. 'Warm' contacts include chums, friends, pals and buddies—people you know. 'Cold' prospects are those you are targeting but who do not qualify as 'warm' yet. The system is fully automated to help you out and make your life easier. Yet, it never worked for me. I'm not sure why. I liked the app, but I never used it to its full potential.

Events and celebrations

Every MLM company runs events. It's in their DNA. They use them for training and annual grand celebrations with more glitz than The Pussycat Dolls' hot-pants. They are also for—and there's no way to break this to you gently—re-programming. It is brainwashing if you prefer.

The owners sometimes made a rock-star style appearance at these events. The company used them to wheel out new products. Associates took inspiration from and were encouraged by brand spanking new promotions, causing them to work twice as hard. Music blared frantically. People bounced around like punk rockers in a mosh pit. I preferred to look on from a dark corner rather than join in. I had just spent the last hour 'Sweaty-Stranger-Hugging' — an act punishable by flogging in parts of the middle-east, I understand, and my inner party-pooper had surfaced to seize control.

Many people attend these events to explore and possibly step outwith the confines of their comfort zone. Everybody felt inspired by the millionaire guest speakers and wanted to be them. Me too. A character played by actor and comedian, Groucho Marx, once said that he had 'worked himself up from nothing to a state of extreme poverty.' I know I am repeating myself, but that's how it felt. The company millionaires who came to beat their chests about their success had exceeded Groucho's less than meteoric trajectory to fame and fortune, but I certainly hadn't.

Still, the stories of their journeys were interesting. Many didn't have a pot to piddle in when they started. They existed on the breadline to give heart, soul, and in a few cases, their liver and kidneys too, to embrace the opportunity the company offered them. Now on these gala nights, they strolled on stage to address thousands of people. They pulled down five-figure monthly paychecks. These exalted few breathed pure oxygen from the top of Mount Olympus. They were no stranger to the spa resorts of Palm Beach or the beaches of Goa. They lived the dream they'd earned.

The company website, YouTube, and Vimeo had stories on every company millionaire. They held me spellbound. Many were genuinely inspirational, relatable, but I still didn't know what they did to get there. Yes, we all had the same opportunity. We all had the same tools. But I'm a visual person. Show me, don't instruct me and expect me to snap my heels and say, 'Sir, yes Sir!'. I needed to be shown in practice so that I can emulate best practice.

One time, a newcomer was on the stage who grossly exaggerated how easy it was to climb the ranks and earn top money with the compensation plan. She claimed to have replaced her 5-figure income within a month of joining our company by dint of our generous compensation package and copious amounts of get-up-and-go on her part.

This claim came before she wrapped the story up by saying she left her previous MLM company, where she was the top income earner, joined ours, and you can guess how she managed to climb the ranks. Yep, half her chums, all from her former company, sat in the front row, cheering her on. How astute of her. Instead of having to sign up new associates faster than a recruiting sergeant on the eve of a major war. Her chums had all lifted their petticoats and leapt into this woman's lifeboat before she rowed away. Naughty girl!

I was fascinated to observe how desperate some attendees were to climb onto that stage. I lacked the guts to do it at the time. I could think of nothing worse than addressing a mass audience—though I suppose discovering that a family of fruit bats had colonised my airing cupboard might qualify. It takes me all my time to cope with a group of familiar friends, to be fair. I need only open my mouth to speak, and I succumb to an episode of the galloping heeby-jeebies. Discomfort permeates every fibre of my being. Perhaps that explained these people's desire to get on stage; they saw it as a way to propel themselves beyond the warmth and stability of their comfort zone.

My long-life ambition was always to become a secret millionaire, an anonymous philanthropist. Like Wonder Woman, I want to be able to help wherever help is needed. How cool would that be? Ahh, well, dreaming never hurts anybody. I should pin that to my vision board.

Chapter 4

MONKEY SEE MONKEY DO

In which Peggy seeks selfies with some super millionaires — fills her weekends with special events — Practises ice-breaking conversations on keeping Vietnamese Pot-bellied pigs as pets — embraces one too many sweaty Herberts for her liking.- Has doubts and fears (though not necessarily in that order) — gets her theme song - tries to sleep with her eyes open (and fails) — starts zooming!

What? No Epiphany bounce?

I slavishly read the posts of a millionairess I was following on Facebook. Though not the only one, I devoured her posts as soon as they appeared. I listened to her Facebook 'lives'. I mean, I practically stalked her.

Once, she posted a video. A recording of her FB live stream, probably. That video had a profound effect on me. I finally understood the opportunity on offer. Her story sounded remarkably similar to mine—before she made her millions, of course! She wanted a life of purpose. She wanted to heal the world. The environment had become a passion of hers, and she, too, wanted to be financially free so she could help where the need arose.

In her youth, she engaged in a frank conversation with her then-boss. She told her superior how unfair she felt the world was; how we must save the environment, stop global warming, turning our green planet into a smoking grey cinder. In short, she told him all about the things about which every young, ambitious feminist girl feels strongly. And this is what her boss said:

'So, what are you going to do about it—chain yourself to a Giant Redwood tree in protest? Refuse to wear lipstick on Wednesdays? That'll not get you a centimetre nearer your dreams.'

That is when she realised how much of a gift this MLM opportunity was. And she decided to do whatever it took to max out the compensation plan and earn as much as possible. After all, money talks. I do not know what she does with her money, but with her passion, I have no doubt she moves mountains, rock by rock. I still check her Facebook occasionally.

Did I experience a post-Epiphany bounce? Was I moved to follow in her golden footsteps? Er...no!

Yet my fascination for the occupants of the company's millionaire's row continued unabated. I have photos with many of them from various events. And before you ask, I didn't suddenly leap from being a wallflower to being Kim Basinger at a film premiere. All I did was join the queue, stand next to them, smile. I took the obligatory selfie and made way for the next buffoon to have their picture taken. They should have painted a circle on the floor with the words' For Buffoons Only' written inside. I proudly posted these pics on my social media wall. It was a way of bragging. Look! Here's me standing next to a millionaire—and I will be next! Given the current velocity of my MLM career, I'd probably have to wait until the next life. I better start looking for a religion that offers one.

'Special' Trainer

Special 'educational weekend events' took place, with exceptional trainers like Richard. On Friday nights only, these were reserved mainly for high performers or those of a certain rank. Richard may well have been the most positive person on the planet. He reminded me of the American Major General from the Korean War in 1950, who was asked by the press corps why his troops were retreating. His reply made headline news: 'Gentlemen; we are not retreating. We are merely advancing in another direction.'

Charming, knowledgeable, with answers for everything, his training spanned an entire weekend. Richard met high-fliers and those beginning to spread their wings impressively, as already mentioned on Friday evenings for extra training.

For reasons which, by now, should be blindingly obvious, I never got to sit in on any of these meetings. I was never even invited to stand at the back. They might as well have hung a sign above the entrance that read 'No Losers Beyond This Point!'

The un-chosen

The rest of us—the un-chosen—started Saturday morning from 9-5. I attended events in Manchester, London and Birmingham. Richard's presentations were jam-packed with material that blew my mind. This stuff was on a par with Penn and Teller making a live elephant disappear on stage.

First of all, unlike many other speakers, he never taught anything he didn't do himself, and that was refreshing in itself. I felt jealous that I wasn't a free spirit like him, that my life wasn't brimming over like his was. But I certainly learnt a lot about myself and felt inspired to do better with my life.

Richard had gained notoriety for pairing a whole room up with strangers. He'd have everyone hugging the living daylights out of each other like long lost friends, meeting for the first time in twenty years. Then, within minutes, everyone would find common ground with the partner he imposed upon us.

The exercise demonstrated the ease with which anyone could be open, friendly and inviting and make new friends. As you now know, I'm not a hugger. But even though I'm not the Greta Thunberg type, I'd rather hug a forest, tree by tree, than embrace a sweaty stranger.

Unrealistic question marathon

However, since many attendees were of the same calibre as me, I played along because if I wanted to network with people for my network marketing business, I needed to change. The snag was, I didn't think I could approach a random stranger on the streets, hug him until he could barely draw breath, and start a conversation about how many Vietnamese Pot-Bellied Pigs I kept as pets.

For me, these exercises often turned into an unrealistic marathon of questions to quickly find common ground, and it went like this:

'I have a dog. Do you have pets?'

'I am married, how about you?'

'Do you have kids? I have two.'

'I like to travel. Do you?'

There was no telling where these random lines of gruelling interrogation might meander before you found something you both had in common. I mean, what next?

'I was born in the Chinese year of the three-toed sloth, what about you?'

'My devil-worshipping Facebook Group celebrates a Black Mass on Zoom on the second Sunday after Lent, what about yours?'

'I like to dress up as a 19th-century Turkish cavalry officer when I make love to my husband; what's your favourite bedroom fantasy?'

Granted, in the room on the day, it kind of worked. We exchanged details, befriended each other on FB as if trophy hunting, and waited for Richard's next set of instructions. He quite often shushed the whole room down because he could not break the audience noise. He always cracked the same joke: 'Three minutes ago, you were all as shy as bush babies. You could barely talk to each other. Now I can't get you to shut up! See how easy this is!'

More annoying than the Go Compare ads

One exercise I hated more than the Go Compare adverts took place during lunch breaks. We had to ring the person we dreaded speaking to most but wanted to talk to about our business. The idea was to call them, leave a voicemail, or connect with them any which way. We all left the room for lunch. Many associates settled for a shake to show their diehard commitment to the company. Others, me amongst them, went to McDonald's or a pub.

When we reconvened, Richard asked how many people we connected with during the break—to the nearest one hundred! Participation, though optional, could be avoided only at a heavy price to your advancement within the ranks.

('You're not taking part, Hazel? That's perfectly okay; just mind the door doesn't swing back and catch your arse on the way out. See ya!')

Non-participation demonstrated an individual's utter lack of the Joan of Arc devotion essential for success in this business.

Richard often joked that his fortune resulted directly from the commitment to change his life. For him, this implied that the reason the rest of us mere mortals still lived on bargain beans and super-saver bread was that we were too scared to venture outside of our comfort zones. I had no problem agreeing with the sentiment expressed, but I lacked the conviction that this indeed was for me.

Did I spend my lunchtime speed-dialling people I dreaded calling? Why would I?

How was this different to ringing somebody today that made my teeth chatter with fear to connect with them on a typical day? 'Hey Sarah, old buddy, old pal. I'm at this amazing event; I really want to talk to you about my weight loss shakes.' As if!

Not only did I have fears, uncertainty and doubts, but they could not make me do things with which I disagreed. I am not them. I do not sound like them. I cannot pretend to be something I am not. There is a difference between being outside of your comfort zone and doing things outside of your moral code.

By this time, the diehard associates, the teacher's pets, had all raised their hands like eager-to-please primary school kids. They hollered at the top of their lungs how many people they'd pursued over lunch. Five! Nine! Twenty-four! 'We have a winner!'

Let me set out my stall here. Girl Guide's honour, I categorically do not have an issue with ambitious people who follow instructions to achieve results. I just can't force myself to comply. You could offer me lunch with Brad Pitt, stuff my pockets with crisp, newly minted tenners, buy me a timeshare in Magaluf, and I'd barely manage to ring my husband or my sister.

Pumping up the jam

The aim of these events was, in part, to pump up, encourage and inspire the associates. They are supposed to show you what is possible to achieve if you are coachable. And that's worth a pause for thought. A weightlifter is still the same weightlifter whether he's pumped up or not. He doesn't change. He doesn't fall behind his sofa like Doctor Jekyll, only to claw his way back to his feet as a hairy-faced, slavering Mr Hyde. The moment you get home, you are you again, back on home turf. Not prepared to put on a show for the rest of your life? No? Then you'll have to dig deep and find your own authentic way to run this business.

Although a reluctant participant—I wouldn't say I went 'all in'—I loved my first training event with Richard. I found him charming and thought-provoking. I was determined to go home, organise my life and implement what I had learnt. I was not ready to start just there and then, but it was time for a change.

An associate's success came down to her team. This was an upline mantra. And this was why uplines repeatedly told associates to bring people to events. Without them, you were Diana Ross without the Supremes. George, Paul and John, minus the bloke that played the drums!

People from the same organisational tree and their leaders packed the room. I caught a glimpse of a few people I recognised from FB groups and my upline's upline. I felt as useless as a one-legged man at an arse-kicking contest. But this prompted the thought that I might just be the first in 'our' tree to hit the big-time. Why not? I was dedicated. I was going to be a 'leader' that swept into the arena thronged by crowds. Then I'd be numero uno, strutting that stage like Beyoncé, inspiring other wannabe associates to up their game ('I've upped my game', I'd say, 'now, up yours!')

One singer, one song

I had already chosen my intro theme song. Some regular speakers bounced on stage to a unique theme tune, like when boxers enter the arena. After a few events, you get to know who's coming up just from listening to their theme song.

I had chosen *It's my life*, by Bon Jovi. It had the edge over the Birdy Song for gravitas, I always thought.

It's my life,

And it's now or never,

I ain't gonna live forever!

I just wanna live while I'm alive!

Pathetic, I know. When else would you live? You won't manage much living when you're dead, will you? Besides, considering I never had the faintest desire for public speaking, selecting an intro tune was getting a little ahead of myself.

'It's no sacrifice!' (Lyrics by Elton John)

Well, excuse me all over the place, Elton, but it bloody well was a sacrifice. As I said, corporate events took place on weekends. Depending on where home, sweet home was for you, it was not unlikely you'd have to travel on Friday night or leave the house in darkness at stupid o'clock on Saturday morning, all so you could save yourself a single night's hotel bill.

The venue for my first ever event was Manchester. Not exactly an intercontinental distance for me to travel, but super inconvenient if I wanted to drive there and back on Saturday, then again on Sunday. I ended up booking the cheapest hotel I could find for that weekend. Who am I kidding? It certainly wasn't a hotel in the same league as the George Cinq in Paris or the Grand Floridian at Disneyland, Florida. It was closer to the kind of Soup Kitchen where you wiped your feet on the way out. Was it a hostel, then? Geez, I don't know. The fact was that it was above an old beer-stained pub in a Manchester suburb. My room had an outside toilet (just joking, but almost! There was a communal toilet on the floor.)

Through a hedge backwards. Twice.

The place made me ill at ease. I tried sleeping with my eyes open but failed. The bedding was clean, but the rest of the room looked as dodgy as a homeless shelter. The shower cubicle was inside the room—very Jasper Conran (Not!). The window had been wedged open in 1958 and never closed again. It faced a major crossroads, so you would have had more chance of catching some shuteye sleeping in a park on Guy Fawkes night.

Everything looked on the verge of falling to pieces. But that was my budget and a good life lesson. I promised myself this was the last time I travelled and slept super- economy. One day, when I became an MLM millionaire, I'd be sharing this silly experience from an executive suite in the Hilton Hotel with the latest cohort of wannabe millionaires, head back, hooting with laughter and trying not to choke on my Veuve Clicquot.

I deliberately avoided taking food with me on the trip, so I drank my convenient meal replacement shake for breakfast, got ready and left to attend the event. When I got back in the evening, I drank my dinner shake, brushed my teeth carefully to avoid accidentally swallowing any of the tap water because this felt like a third-world country accommodation. When I finally fell asleep, it was to a commotion from drunks downstairs. I imagined this was what it was like sleeping in an Iraqi jail. Mornings I looked like a mess — as if some farmer, with a tractor, had dragged me through a hedge backwards. Then, unsatisfied with the result, driven back around the front again for a second go.

Fake it 'til you make it

My next event the following year was in the London Hilton Hotel. No, of course, I wasn't staying there. I remained light-years from the millionaire status I coveted. Besides, with more expenses to pay this time to travel further for an event, I was lucky to get myself two nights in a hotel near Victoria Station.

The room was a little bigger than a laundry basket. I asked at the desk if I could borrow a cat to swing, but the receptionist said there was no room for such a manoeuvre. When I opened my arms, I could touch both sides of the room with ease. But it was a nice clean place in a relatively safe area. Plus, I had my very own toilet, so it felt like I was moving up in the world.

I finally made it to the Hilton hotel for the Birmingham celebrations. They'd discounted the room, and even though it was still expensive for my pocket, it was super reasonable for that kind of luxury, so I had treated myself. 'Fake it until you make it.'

Buddy, can you spare a dime

I was still skint, by the way, no further up the greasy pole than at the time of the previous event. I received periodic payments from the few people that signed up under me, but that was all.

Here's how it worked: when my downline ordered their products, I received a credit on my account. Once I accumulated enough points to trigger a payment, I received forty quid! Slaughter the fatted calf! Let loud Hosannas ring out across the land! The more points I accumulated, the more forty quid payments I received. I wasn't complaining, but I wasn't covering my monthly grocery bill. Yes, I made enough to feed a family of four—a family of field mice, that is.

To be included in the compensation plan, you had to be active. The minimum order in points came to approximately £120 worth of products. On top of that, my husband was a downline customer, requiring him to make that minimal order too. However, if you wanted to lose weight which was our objective, we had to spend close to £300; twice!

Let me just show you the money here. My forty quid covered the monthly fees of the fancy apps. The rest got devoured by my overdraft. The was a blossoming sum, which, on its current trajectory, threatened to swell to the size of the National debt of Somalia. On the debit side, I had two kids, and a dog (or was that the other way round? I was so busy I often got confused.) I was honour-bound to feed all of these entities. Then you had our shake order, and I still had to find the money for an excellent nutritional dinner which, of course, wasn't in powdered form.

Zoom meetings, Skype meetings, Facetime

Lots of leaders held weekly Zoom meetings for their team and potential prospects. My upline and her upline would invite me to Zoom meetings at 10 pm on Thursdays because one of the other associates on the call was in a US time zone, and that was the only time to get us all on the same call without some poor sod having to wear a nightie on screen.

I am half-dead by half-past eight because I have a full-time job and often get up at half-five (apologies for the heavy use of simple fractions there), but I joined the calls feeling determined to crack the code.

These calls eventually fizzled out like a dying firework leaving me to plough a lone furrow. Even though I knew I could always reach out for help, it was not the same if the leader did not lead by example. I don't mean to criticise my upline in any way, it just wasn't for them, or they found different priorities. No hard feelings. I'm saying that it's hard to copy something when you don't have an excellent example from which to copy.

Asia zooms

However, somebody above my upline's upline from another country reached out to me because they acknowledged my enthusiasm for this and invited me to join the Asia zoom calls. Exciting times! Her calls took place every Sunday with a much bigger audience, with some participants from different countries—to start with at least.

Something wasn't right. I could feel it in my water. Like an ill-fitting wig, the call just didn't sit right. I felt lectured to, read a sermon even. You know that feeling when you sense that the words spoken did not chime with the underlying (and actual) message?

The more I got to know the leader—a lovely lady, by the way—the less able I felt to relate to her. It became apparent to me that she was going to walk past dead bodies to become a millionaire. I wonder how she's getting on; maybe she's made it by now.

Her upline had recently been revealed as the latest millionaire, putting even more spring in her step. She inhabited every social platform, messaging people, meeting people, cold calling, ordering on people's behalf. She also talked to our friends behind our backs. She needed the orders, the points to keep the payments rolling in.

I should explain, an MLM millionaire is not somebody who has one million pounds in her account. Instead, this is someone whose accumulated sales reached the million mark. As you rose through the ranks, you were paid weekly for the orders people underneath you had made. You also get paid daily and monthly bonuses and percentages of your teams' performance.

I can't say how it worked because I failed to make it past the rank of consultant. Anyone interested enough to explore the exact arithmetic of the scheme should study the compensation plan thoroughly. Every company will have an official version of the compensation videos, especially if they wish to attract business builders to their organisations. Many wannabe millionaires launch their own YouTube video or a Vimeo to get their name out there.

I may be thicker than the Greater Los Angeles phone book, I suppose. I grasped the basic principle, and I suspect that eventually, the penny would drop once the money started to hit my account. Alas, as I never progressed, I just read about it and pretended I understood.

Chapter 5

UNCHAIN MY HEART (AND THROW MY WORKSTATION INTO A SKIP WHILE YOU'RE AT IT!)

In which Peggy embraces the age-old parental advice, 'Do not as I do, do as I say!' — Spends 24/7 on her mobile phone and feels like a candidate for Child Abandoner of the Year — Practises excuses to withhold essential information from interested clients — Lives with the shame of having 'uncoachable' stamped on her forehead — Grasps the answer to the MLM FAQ, 'When is a pyramid scheme not a pyramid scheme?' As 'When asked if it is, of course!'

Not only did you wave goodbye to the concept of free time at evenings and weekends, you ended up habitually doing what you expressly forbade your children from doing—spending every waking moment on your mobile.

The infinitive number of FB groups I joined, the successful people I stalked, the best MLM coaches from different MLM companies I followed, the questions from the private groups. Ping! Always another notification on my phone. I regretted befriending my boss on FB. When she hung around on FB during business hours, she would have seen the amount of time I spent on social media. Early-onset FOMO gripped me. I felt compelled to find out what was said. All my replies had to be immediate. We were programmed to chase and reply proactively, to keep the momentum going whatever it took.

The mothership awaits

Simultaneously, any response to a clickbait item associates posted about the company was to earn an enigmatic answer. To the question, 'What is it?' The standard response was to say any of the following:

'Sorry, I'm busy right now. I'm making chilli con carne; I will message you later.' What would we say when we'd exhausted our stock of plausible responses? When we ran out of ways to delay client gratification?

'My llama is poorly today; I'll call you when I return from the vet.'

Or, 'As a member of the Kidsgrove E.T. Skygazers, I will spend most of the day on a Welsh mountainside waiting for the mothership to land and take us back to the Andromeda galaxy where we belong. I'll call you if it's another false alarm (it usually is).'

On what planet do you create curiosity only to say, 'sorry, I'm busy'? Maybe it's me. Perhaps I am what's known to MLM insiders as (enter SFX of thunder and lightning on a biblical scale) un-coachable?

Not the Big 'C'

'Give it to me straight doc, what's wrong with me?'

'Well, I don't know how to break this to you—'

'Is it the big C?'

'No, not that.'

'Come on, doc, help me out here. How long have I got to live?'

'Now, now, stop crying. You'll probably live to see your telegram from the queen.' A pregnant pause, then more biblical thunder, followed by, '—but you will never be coachable until the end of your days!'

These annoying delays in communication with the very people you are desperate to recruit might go down well with those in professions different from mine. But the day jobs of corporate world inhabitants like me are all-consuming. So when you post to social media before work, you will get some traction during the day because who goes on FB at 6 am to get curious about shakes? Only flat-earthers and those who believe Elvis never died, that's who.

Not now

Some of my colleagues, forward slash, friends have signed up (they were also my FB friends), so it felt doubly awkward because they got notifications when I posted. They were in the product-user group because I invited them. There was no escaping, and I couldn't take advantage. I worked for a company that paid me and trusted me to do my job in 'day' hours. So every spare moment I was at home, I found myself staring down at my smartphone screen with the intensity of a hypnotist gazing into the eyes of a patient—learning, scrolling, liking, commenting, getting notices. I feared turning into an absentee mother as my catchphrases became, 'Not now, I'm busy' and 'I've got to do this, wait' And all the while barely making eye contact with the very people I loved more than anything—well at that time, nearly anything.

The company hid nothing from us here. They explicitly told us that sacrifices must be made, especially at the beginning. We would reap our rewards later, and our families would thank us for it.

I didn't think my family would thank me at that stage—maxing out my credit card with monthly orders to stay active. I was a busy mummy but an absent wife. And on top of all this, I felt as if I had sown no seeds at all. I did not realise that 'busy' and 'productive' have two vastly different meanings. Multitasking is not smart either. To achieve your goals, I think you should focus on one thing at a time. But this was all part of the learning, and in my case, telling me was never going to be enough—I had to live it, experience it, feel it.

However, the leader's best thigh-slapping remark had to be this one: Even if you have a full-time job, you surely have 15 minutes in a day. (Pause while I split my sides). Fifteen minutes was all it took, they said. Develop your business in small pockets of your time. Your lunchtime, for instance!

Sorry, Jose – you're not on

This made me so angry I could have crushed a marshmallow with one hand. In my book, building a mighty network marketing business, connecting with people, getting to know them—part of which must indeed involve answering their questions, cannot be achieved in 15 minutes a day. You could do the washing-up or cram in a bit of Tai Chi in these illusive quarters of an hour. But do anything that creates value to your fledgeling MLM enterprise? No way, Jose!

There's no point in arguing with me about this. I'd only stamp my feet and drum my dainty fists off my home office desk until you backed down or ran away. I'll concede that it's possible to message a template to five people in 15 mins. You can have that. The problem is that surely you message them as a prelude to a conversation, right? You want to build relationships. So what's to be done if they reply immediately? Do you ignore them? I can't buy that. Maybe I am (cue thunder for the last time) un-coachable.

If you can't focus, how about accountability calls?

A leader in a UK WhatsApp group extended a welcome to one and all to join her Zoom call from 6.30 am – 7 am. I scratched my head when she said these were silent calls. Nobody talked, and there was no discussion. I learnt that the purpose of these calls was to demonstrate accountability. To commit to daily activities for one half-hour.

When you dialled into the Matrix, you remained on mute, and just cracked on with what you needed to do—write out your daily shopping list, groom the dog, give yourself an Indian head massage. Of course, if moonlighting as a shepherdess to make ends meet, you couldn't nip out to rescue wayward members of your flock from vertigo-inducing ledges with your shepherdess's crook because you had to stay on screen. Other than that, the world was, as I remarked earlier, your lobster.

I suppose this could work for those struggling with focus, but I have to have autonomy or don't feel right. On reflection, was this another element of personal failure? Refusing the helping hand? There are many ways to get things done, and life demands that we find them, but procrastination isn't one of them.

Epiphany II! The sequel.

And then came my second epiphany! Objections! I finally learnt the truth about myself in one of the presentations by—you guessed it—a company millionaire. He happened to be one of my favourite guys in the organisation. He reached deep down into my soul and answered all the questions for which non-movers like me thirsted. He said: 'You cannot deal with other people's objections until you get rid of your own.'

My head lit up like a Vegas slot machine paying out on a million-dollar jackpot.

It seemed so clear at that moment. Think about it, in the absence of any objections; you would talk about your opportunity with the ease of a talk-show host. You would be unstoppable. Everyone that crossed your path would receive a powerful, lucid message stemming from your unqualified support for the product. Let's face it; it would be downright criminal not to tell your story.

I had top-class products. I had seen the health of thousands improve. People lost weight that had stubbornly refused to shift for years. And they felt great. Some significantly improved their finances, some had an excellent second income whilst others took it to the next level and made this their sole income, earning money beyond their wildest dreams.

I repeatedly told my husband that I refused to give up. There was money on the table. I just had to grab it. But my objections froze me with fear and rendered me unable to share.

He found it easy to talk about it at work. I am pretty sure he spoke to more people than I did in my workplace! Yet, I could not shake off the feeling that I was selling when I wanted to share. As my mind-beam swept across the populace and occasionally fell on any random salad-dodger, I immediately thought that a poor person needed to lose weight and immediately became a member of my target audience.

Oiling the entrepreneurial wheels

Everybody agreed that not all weight-challenged people wanted to look like Cindy Crawford or David Beckham. And they instructed us to build relationships with prospects by listening, not pouncing on them like a squirrel on a monkey nut, immediately revealing our true motives.

We did not lack examples of MLM jargon to oil the wheels of our entrepreneurial machines.

'Listen until your ears hurt.'

'ABC – Always Be Curious.'

'Just listen to their problems; it could be they have an issue with sleep or energy, it is not always about the excess weight. Losing weight comes as a bonus.'

'Facts tell, stories sell.'

'If they have a price objection, show them the value. Price is absent in the presence of value.'

Well, no shit, Sherlock. I got that. I may be un-coachable, but I'm not stupid. I recognised the destination. I just didn't yet know which train would take me there.

Sigh

Your job is to make the prospect realise that they cannot afford not to get your product. Our duty was to demonstrate that if the prospect shared with two people, who also got started on the products, they would recoup the cost of their first month immediately.

This sounded terrific. Yet still, that cautionary voice rang out in my head. How could I approach my friends and say 'come and join me', knowing full well that my shakes were as yet unpaid? I pretended not to have a financial objection when in reality, I did. It was an endless battle.

Don't overthink it, they said. You are doing them a favour by sharing this opportunity to get these beautiful products. Keeping this to ourselves would be a profoundly selfish act.

Objections a-go-go

Prospects objected all right. About price. About ingredients. They were uneasy about whether or not this was a pyramid scheme and about autoship*. 'It's not the right time,' they'd say. Or 'I like real food.' The company had an answer to every objection you could imagine. And here we return to the start of my doubts: How could I give convincing answers to the prospects' questions if I did not believe them?

Not believing bought me a one-way ticket to Nowhere City, Nebraska. Because a failure to convincingly dismiss common objections was always unlikely to result in a Disney-style line of people desperate to sign up for my MLM roller coaster. The Good Book had it right: Oh ye of little faith!

(*Autoship: A scheme in MLM where people sign up to have products shipped on a fixed date every month. The advantage to signatories is a 25% discount on qualifying orders.)

At coaching sessions and on Zoom calls, leaders often told associates that they needed to take the business seriously. They got no argument from me on that score. Treating MLM as a hobby was a doomed enterprise. Must-haves for success included daily task lists, weekly goals, 90-day look-ahead and constant progress checks. Like a shark, you needed to remain in continuous motion, or your dream would die on you.

But procrastination is a bitch, and as we have already established, 'busy' isn't a synonym of 'productive'. In a bricks-and-mortar business with an upfront investment, you wouldn't think twice. You would have worked your little cotton socks off to make it a success.

Whalebone corsets and Sherbet Dabs

But since you can get started in MLM for little more than the cost of your grocery budget (you basically 'eat your overhead'), you don't take it as seriously. This situation is entirely unlike a traditional business, like a flower shop. Or one of those Open All Hours corner shops that sell everything from whalebone corsets to Sherbet Dabs, both of which would have needed to take out business loans to get their corsets and Sherbet Dabs off the ground (if you catch my drift.)

This was especially true in my case, as my monthly salary wasn't exactly shabby. I didn't have to beat the wolves back from my cabin door with a cast-iron skillet. Nor did I have one of those 9-5 jobs where you started to lose the will to live at 09:05, emotionally imploded by lunchtime and by 15:10 had become catatonic with boredom and resentment.

Still, I desperately wanted to tunnel out of this prison and stride out into virgin territory.

I craved the financial freedom everybody talked about. The kind of freedom that would allow me to do stuff that meant a lot to me: Trample through a Guatemalan rainforest, Swim the length of Lake Titicaca without the aid of flippers, gift my husband the early retirement he deserves, being my own boss and spending more time with my children. However, motivation is more challenging to muster than herding cats when the rewards just weren't there whilst keeping my full time, demanding job.

The highest MLM fliers in my neighbourhood earned far less money than I brought home from my day job, and I saw how hard they worked for that. The identities of many wandered off at some ill-defined stage of the process of their assimilation into MLM and never came back.

Your soul laid bare at 56 Mb/sec

Any privacy they started with gradually evaporated like morning fog on a scorcher of a day. Non-stop posting on every known online medium laid bare every facet of their lives at 56Mb per second: The name of their pet tortoise, the date of their first body piercing, and the number and location of every tattoo.

This was not my dream job, after all. Thanks, but no thanks! I did not sign up for that. I wanted a business I could build in the pocket of my own time and bathe in money as everybody promised.

The trickiest question of all

If asked, 'Is this a Pyramid scheme?' you were supposed to come back with, 'Would it be ok if I defined a pyramid scheme for you? It is an illegal scheme, where they have no products to sell. Besides, I would never be involved in anything illegal.' Or you could simply ask them to explain to you what they believed a Pyramid scheme to be. This struck me as what linguists refer to PVV (Patronising Verbal Vomit).

The most perplexing issue around the whole 'Pyramid Scheme-Not Pyramid Scheme' experience manifests itself whenever you attempt to illustrate the compensation plan to somebody.

'This is YOU, here at the top. You share with two friends, one of which is on the left and the other on the right underneath you. Then friend A shares with two more friends, who also has one on the left and one on the right underneath him. And your friend B who also shares with two friends. She also has one on the left and one on the right underneath her...'

Commit this schematic to paper, and very soon, you will be looking at a pyramid shape with you at the apex. It's inevitable—a mathematical certainty.

I can't honestly say my company was a pyramid scheme. They sold many products and recruited differently than other MLM companies. I simply found the compensation plan a bit curious.

Shake, rattle and roll

If a prospect said, 'I don't want to drink shakes,' they expected us to throw it right back at them and ask, 'So what are you doing to reach your personal goals?' We'd carpet-bomb them with nutrition fact after nutrition fact until the noise deafened them. 'Do you have any idea how many nutrients you get in one meal replacement shake?' We'd retort, attack being the best form of defence. 'Compared to your so-called regular produce from over-farmed, over-fertilised fields of genetically modified beetroot lying under a permanent haze of butterfly-murdering pesticide, blah-blah-blah.'

And if you failed to convince them that time, you let them get on with their lives. Only, you ambushed them later under the guise of checking up on their progress, and firing the MLM Exocet missile of patronising questions: 'How is stacking shelves at ASDA working out for you, huh?'

And finally, the 'time' objection. No, I don't mean anyone objected to time as a dimension. I'm on about the classic, 'I don't have time for this MLM malarkey, guv.' Take five while I haul on my best pair of smarty pants and do a Carol Vorderman number on you:

'How many hours are there in a week?'

'24 hours x 7 days equal 168 hours.'

'We all have 168 hours.'

'Count 8 hrs a day for sleep, forty hours work, four hours of pilates and high-impact jazzercise (including the warm down), fourteen for family, friends, and feeding ant eggs to the goldfish.'

'Tot that lot up, subtract the first number you thought of, and you still come out with fifty-four hours a week of spare time to build your business.'

'If you stopped watching Netflix and gave the mindless scrolling on social media a body swerve, you absolutely would have time.'

Whoa! What a condescending response. At this point, those considered the wisest in the company was as coherent as Yoda.

'An objection was a request for information. No, it wasn't!

'An objection was a fear of something new, wasn't it?' Not In my case, it wasn't!

I believe objection is an excuse to shut you up. Or have a good argument to see you squirm. People often like to play cruel games with brainwashed MLM reps just for fun.

Give it to me straight doc, what's wrong with me?
Well, I don't know how to break this to you...
Is it the Big C? No, not that. Come on doc, help me out
here,. How long have I got to live? Now, now, stop crying.
You'll probably live to see your telegram from
the queen............ But you will never be coachable
until the end of your days!

Chapter 6

LOSERS ALONE REINVENT THE WHEEL; I'M GOING TO BE A COPYCAT.

In which: Peggy embraces self-denial, refusing to believe that the kilocalories burned before succeeding in MLM exceed those expended by Scott of the Antarctic when he man-hauled his sledge to the South Pole — Wonders if 'Why? Why? Seven times why?' comes from a Shakespearean play — Looks on, slack-jawed in amazement at her upline's upline's upline's capacity to fall asleep in the shower, while recruiting on her mobile phone — experiences the three-way call and voodoo accounting.

Simple, but hard

Simple. But hard. A definition of John Rambo? No. These words described one of the most profound lessons taught to MLM disciples. It sounded as simple as a temple bell—You followed a proven formula, walked a path much trodden by the many who came before you. There were few if any reasons to reinvent any wheels here when we had everything we needed at our fingertips. I could do this, I thought, but then that was the simple part.

The hard part would not have sounded out of place if described by Mr Miyagi from the movie Karate Kid: The hard part was both obvious and yet simultaneously unknown. The hard part would have completely confused Confucius.

I noticed how little fellow associates shared their struggles*. Nobody ever admitted how hard they actually worked for fear that nobody would want to join them. There they were trying to sell you a fantastic opportunity to make passive income that flowed into your bank account while you slept, as easily as the Mississippi flowed down to the Gulf of Mexico.

(*I mean that normal sized associates seldom shared their struggles. Not that dwarf associates shared their struggles. Just saying.)

No rush for the abacus

'You get out what you put in,' they said, but seriously, nobody rushed to their abacus to calculate the actual number of hours they put in day and night because the idea was to build your massive organisation in the there-and-gone pockets of your spare time: while your children slept, while frantically munching your way through a lunchtime Pret A Manger Croque Monsieur like a neurotic chinchilla. Or, God helps you while waiting for a bus.

Sigh

This is where I tell you about the clever MLM stuff. Pour yourself a shot of tequila if you can. You'll need a stiffener to survive the next few paragraphs.

'What's your WHY?'

'WHY do you want to lose weight?' It isn't because you're determined to get into a dress that looks like it's been sprayed onto a size zero fashion model.

'WHY do you need to improve your sleep?' It isn't because you've got less energy than a hedgehog fresh from hibernation.

'WHY do you want to make lots of money?' It's not because you want to wear more bling than Jay Z.

Granted, those are the first answers that spring to mind when asked the WHY question. But, according to those gifted in psych-babble, your first answer is never the real reason. (You'd be excused for having your own comeback to any of these irritating questions. Something like, 'WHY is your nose all over your face? It isn't because I've nutted you, you annoying MLM muppet—Oh! Hold on! Yes, it is!')

A method exists to discover somebody's actual 'Why.' It can be compared to the peeling of a pickled onion (for the pukka way to carry out this manoeuvre, see Delia Smith.) You ask somebody 'Why' seven times, never accepting their first answer. Essentially, you keep peeling the layers off that pickled onion by repeatedly asking why. Until, like somebody who has binge-watched three back-to-back omnibus episodes of Eastenders, you holler, 'Enough already!' And give up the real answer— possibly whilst sobbing.

It would be easy to conclude that these prospects were lying. Or that they were avoiding answering the question. They quite often didn't know themselves at the beginning of the conversation. And it came as a genuine surprise to them when they discovered their real why.

This was often a poignant experience for the prospect. They might end up with their lip wobbling like the mudguard of a moped doing 50 KPH against the prevailing wind. The point of digging this deep was to connect them to their ultimate 'why' emotionally. Later, if they were backsliding, you could always 'hold them to account' for this inner truth (those who call a spade a spade might use the word 'blackmail').

This method worked most of the time on most prospects. It did not, however, work on me when my upline's upline questioned me about my why. I am a deep thinker, but I don't share many of my deep thoughts and desires with passers-by, people who happen to be behind me in the deli queue, or opportunistic Jehovah's Witnesses who pitch up on my doorstep.

Maybe I didn't know my true why at the time. I just knew I wanted more money to live. I finally learnt my 'why' at an event where the method was demonstrated: 'I want to be in control!'

Bullseye! There it was—my why. I wanted to answer to no one. I didn't want to be dependent on anybody; I didn't want to ask my boss if I could, pretty please, go on holiday. I didn't ever want to tell my kids we couldn't afford stuff. I wanted to live, not just exist. Life was too short to work, sleep, repeat.

I had two kids I saw only at breakfast and dinner. I had been a mortgage slave for 15 years, paying for a house seldom I lived in because I was always at work. There were so many beautiful places on Earth, and I could only afford to go on holiday once a year if I put it on a credit card. I was grateful for what I had, and I knew it was loads more than many people would ever have, but this opportunity could make my dreams come true.

And you know what? Sitting here, writing this book, my dominant feeling right now is guilt. I feel guilty about my unfulfilled dream. Unfulfilled because I couldn't conjure up the passion for my 'why'. Why didn't I want to be in control? It didn't make sense. After all, this was the only objective in my life.

I had a less complicated take on this. Perhaps this business model just wasn't for me. It's one thing to know somebody with a cool job—we all know at least one of those— but that says nothing about whether the same job would be cool for us too. There should be an area set aside in the window of every employment agency for a sign that says, 'Cool job vacancies, available—apply within.'

30-second story

What MLM associates in my company called the thirty-second story, others might call an elevator pitch. The idea is that if you had only the time, it took for an elevator to take you to the top floor of a building, could you pitch your opportunity to the person next to you, concisely and effectively? It's not easy, in those thirty seconds, to convince a cold prospect to enrol in a course of 30 Lucozade enemas.

We had tools to help us. Such as a handy template of what to include in our stories, though it was basically a summary of what the product or the opportunity did for you.

We were taught to be truthful and never to claim our products treated or prevented disease. They urged us not to over-promise or offer guarantees (If regularly chewing my product doesn't give you the libido of a Bonobo monkey, I'll give you the deeds to my house.) Remain accurate and give reasonable expectations, they advised. The essential idea was to describe your life before you started. To reveal who gave you the opportunity. To say for how long you'd used the products or run your business.

Then, as a result of the products or the opportunity—and here you filled in with any attention-grabbing narrative you could muster (you became an Olympic swimmer, the first pan-sexual on the Space Station, or the first woman body-builder that could crack walnuts between the cheeks of her arse, and so on.)

The problem was if you wanted to start this business from the word go, you had no thirty-second story to tell. In this case, we were advised to use somebody else's story. Not for the first time, I felt uncomfortable about this. It was disingenuous. But it made perfect sense.

Whether or not you took this path very much depended on your personality. If you were serious about building your business with speed, you would do it, but elegantly. I felt incapable of this level of deception (was that too strong a word?) which was why I frantically sought my own thirty-second story.

Associates were not limited to a single story. You could have many different stories for as many different circumstances and different prospects because, of course, not everybody wanted to lose weight, become a millionaire, or experience the dubious pleasures of a Lucozade enema.

I hoped to attract people to the opportunity—the more business builders in your downline, the quicker you'd attain your goals. Great! But how do you entice anyone to rally around your flag when you were still light years away from earning enough to buy your own products? A classic catch 22.

Leaders rehearsed their stories on stage, encouraging associates to do the same. In practice, most speakers preferred to start by sharing their story before training. After taking the products for a few months, I finally had my own story (Hooray!) I had two, come to think of it. The first told how I lost a whopping 20lb in 3 months and how I had not felt that lean and healthy since Claudia Schiffer strutted down the catwalk for the first time.

My second story was even better. My digestive system was like new. For obvious reasons, I wouldn't say I liked to share this story because nobody wants to talk about guts. Unless, of course, you get a prospect that struggles with their digestive system.

ASSOCIATE: 'Let me tell you, since I lost 20 pounds, I have been passing stools like World War Two torpedoes!'

PROSPECT: 'Wow, that's incredible! That's been my ambition for years. Where do I sign?'

A gross exaggeration, of course, but to this day, I remain extremely grateful for the health improvement in my life.

The thirty-second story I most wanted, though, was about the money potential presented by this opportunity. The problem was another facet of the catch 22 mentioned earlier. I was earning less from the business at that time than a Bolivian peasant farmer. And that's how it would stay until I tempted more people to my downline, to either buy my products or become a rep. I wasn't prepared to share my uplines' uplines' upline's epic tale about how she now pulled down a four-figure monthly income because I was already earning that from my corporate job.

My upline's upline's upline

In my mind, I was not improving my financial situation because my uplines' upline's upline was at it twenty-five hours a day, flaunting her whole life on social media from the moment she woke up to the moment she fell asleep in the shower at night—if, in fact, she did sleep. The woman had no off switch. This wasn't painting a canvas of financial freedom; it was a social media detention centre.

I also noticed that my story never seemed to fit the thirty-second time limit. Like a rogue blackberry bush, it demanded constant pruning. To be effective, I needed to condense it to a short spiel that sounded authentic and flowed effortlessly. Not an awkward 'um, basically I drank the shakes and lost 20 pounds. They tasted awesome, and I highly recommend them,' a spiel with embarrassing, unnatural, and inauthentic pauses.

I would not be writing this book had I been in any way successful at this MLM malarkey; it dawned on me around this time that I might not fit the MLM business model. Although on reflection, perhaps I just hadn't chosen the right company.

Swigging the selling juice

Again, I had not sorted out my own objections and hence never got rid of the feeling of constantly trying to sell. I felt like the central character in Dr Jekyll and Mr Hyde. My true persona was like the good doctor's—pleasant, amiable, thoughtful of my fellow man. Then, at night, the corporate job parked up for the day, one hefty swig of the Selling Juice (£250 a litre (Exc VAT) from MLM stores everywhere) and my inner Mr Hyde threatened to emerge, hairy handed, touting my shakes in dark alleys to anyone who might listen, if only I'd allow him.

My sole motive was to make money, but it was hard for me to shake off the self-imposed stigma of making money from people in one business to use as capital for another. And I never got to thinking, 'OMG, these products are so good, I must tell everyone I meet', even though I had excellent physical results myself.

It was different from other people's 30-second stories—I loved those. It was great to learn of the many improvements in their lives. Insomniacs sleeping like babies, salad dodgers finally shedding the fat they couldn't on the Borscht diet, mental health and brain-fog lifting, migraines evaporating for the first time in months, extra cash to put towards a first family holiday, saved marriages, some really touching stories, real gratitude for the company.

3-way calls

Though no one ever said so in so many words, it was crystal clear to all associates that failure to immerse ourselves in the culture of 3-way calls would result in being placed in a pickled herring barrel and thrown over Niagara Falls. In practice, that meant that if you struck up a conversation or messaged somebody who'd shown even a slight interest in your product or opportunity, you did not let them ask too many questions. You got them on a 3-way call.

You said, 'I have only been doing this for a short while, so let's connect with Anna; she can answer any questions you may have.' By this stage in my story, you will not be surprised to learn that these tri-cornered transactions were extensively covered by rules, templates, voodoo accounting and more self-important wiffle-waffle than you'd hear at an annual convention of extroverts.

In stage one, you invited your prospect to join a conversation with you and your upline. From the outset, you introduce your prospect to your upline by painting a glowing portrait of your upline's prowess and credentials. By the time you are through, the prospect should feel that if they are stupid enough not to engage with your upline and ultimately your opportunity, they should trade their head in for a bowling ball and take a taxi home.

Stage two was devastatingly simple, comprising as it did, a single action requiring virtually no effort at all: you shut the hell up. You were to make less noise than a dormouse preening its whiskers.

You handed the reins of this horse to your upline, who immediately galloped toward your prospect, firing off a barrage of questions. You had one purpose in life at this point—to listen. They used to tell us, 'We were born with two ears and only one mouth. Learn to listen. Always Be Curious (ABC).'

Your upline basically sells for you—based on a script, may I add. Even millionaire trainers told us they still used the script. It kept them on track. You never knew what the prospect would say or might ask that could potentially derail you, so having the script meant you could re-focus immediately. This also proved that scripts worked.

Some prospects point blank refused to go on a three-way call but were willing to be introduced to your 'mentor' either via WhatsApp or Messenger. Not everybody felt comfortable talking to a stranger on the phone, and I couldn't blame them. This allowed them to ask their questions from a safe distance.

In theory, your upline should always be ethical and never start a separate conversation without copying you in, because after all, it is your prospect. In practice, however, it was as common as drizzle in Scotland. Luckily, it never happened to me.

Ultimately, you should get to recruit that person. Your upline was there for support and knowledge, not to steal your prospects. If you were lucky to sign up that prospect, your upline benefited too, since the compensation plan was designed to cause points from any product sales to flow up through the organisation.

Thank you for taking my call. I have this great opportunity for you and I didn't want you to miss out on it...

Chapter 7

FRIENDS, ROMANS, MLM ASSOCIATES, LEND ME YOUR EARS (AND YOUR CONTACT LISTS TOO, IF YOU DON'T MIND.)

In which: Peggy learns that the most popular answer given to clients is 'I dunno.' — Is told to celebrate when a client says 'no.'— gets told that speaking to ten people a day is the least she can do — Learns the horrors of unidentified, unresolved objections.

MLM' friends'

The sun comes up in the east and sets in the west, and MLM consultants befriend other MLM consultants. It's a natural law. Unfortunately, the motivation of some wasn't to befriend me but to swipe my friends' list. Ouch! Who knows how they sniffed me out? MLM people desperate for customers can smell fresh blood as readily as a hyperactive vampire.

Leaders occasionally posted profiles of such predators (and vampires too on one occasion, I think) on our business messenger chat group, with instructions to immediately block them. They had run out of people to talk to, so they'd targeted someone else's friends. Charming.

The quintessential answer

Another thing that boiled my water: I could not get my head around the company's views on prospect questions. These rules, like a French baguette, swallowed sideways, always stuck in my throat. You did not have to be an expert. Material abounded. I could tag them in a Facebook post; I could go on the many official company websites and find the relevant article and send it to them.

Don't try to answer everything. The best answer is 'I don't know'. Is it just me? Or do you read this and cringe too? It's self-evident that not everyone can be an expert, and reading the odd article wouldn't make you one, but letting the prospect read the article for themselves made them accountable for their decisions.

However, if asked about shakes I had taken every day for six months, 'I don't know,' hardly offered a plausible reason to invest in my opportunity. This wishy-washy retort failed to cast you as Confidence Gal (See Marvel comics for details of superpowers, uniform, public holidays, and so on). I suppose it could have been worse:

PROSPECT: So, just how wonderful and life-transforming are these shakes?

ASSOCIATE: I dunno.

PROSPECT: But you've been taking them forever, haven't you? You must have some opinion!

ASSOCIATE: (Shrugs shoulders, considers the state of her nail varnish.)

To my mind, 'I don't know, let me find out' sounded much better. I suppose this was when they expected you to use all the tools and materials at your disposal. That way, you'd avoid giving out wrong information, overpromising or committing to something that turned out to be untrue.

This tactic also helped with duplication because you taught your business builder prospect to do as you did and say, 'I don't know'. This felt too detached and impersonal, especially when I had serious intentions for the business. Besides, why would I mention anything I knew nothing about? That didn't make sense.

Another unwritten rule was always to leverage and take advantage of your upline. Let them do the talking. But what was I supposed to do when I became somebody's upline? At what point did my MLM chakras magically realign with Jupiter, and I rematerialise as the legendary MLM 'guru', Maharishi Fancy-Pants?

When building a network marketing business, my downline would at some point approach me with their prospects for a 3-way call. Do I keep on mithering the same upline to death? If I wanted to do this full time, shouldn't I collect enough knowledge to support my team? I never understood this transition, and nobody was willing to explain it to me.

The Yes/No ratio (No, no, no, no, no, no, no, no, no, yes, no, no, no, no.)

I previously mentioned that part of every event's agenda was earmarked for interviews with successful leaders. During questioning, associates had to count how many people they'd connected with and how many of those had said 'yes' vs 'no'.

There is nothing more disheartening than a potential prospect saying 'no', except maybe losing a tenner and finding a shilling. I think these little demonstrations were supposed to make us proud of hearing the noes*. They told us to celebrate all noes because that meant we were talking to people!

(*And before you start writing letters to my publisher, 'Noes' is the plural of 'no', so get over it)

They said that every successful leader harvested thousands of noes (the chaff) before they got 20 Yeses (the wheat). This was meant to comfort us. The idea that despite hearing 'no' more times than your average teenager says, 'there's never anything to eat in this house,' the millionaires simply moved on.

I suppose it was encouraging to know you were not the only one. Still, it was also discouraging to see that you'd have to mine 31 metric tonnes of rock to recover a single ounce of gold; an associate must speak to 5,000 people to find the few nuggets willing to join them.

Optimism was the beating heart of network marketing. It permitted you to count noes as good things because each additional 'no' took you ever closer to a yes.

When you approach me with this type of schoolboy logic, being a realist, take care I don't lecture your head off your shoulders about the potential for misinterpretation. Take this up the wrong way, and you could end up on a mission to converse with the passionless. You aim to hear as many negative responses as you can, in the slightly off-the-wall belief that only when rejected 342 times could you possibly hear the word 'yes'.

Why not guarantee a no by slapping each new prospect across the size of the head with a freshly landed halibut before you even say hello? (Do not try this at home! Or anywhere else, for that matter; They'll charge you with multiple counts of GBH—something that does not do your CV any good.)

Failure is only nature's way of telling you you're crap

So here I was, adding to my collection of noes, every time I spoke to a new person, the objective being to talk about my opportunity to at least ten people a day—Wait. What?? I had a full-time job. I could not possibly have a conversation with ten people in one day.

I did not see that many 'new' people each day in my office? I saw Karen from HR, Bob from IT and Jane from the facility management regularly.

I thought I saw Elvis late at our Christmas party one year, but I blame the cheap Prosecco for that.

Move over, Pinocchio; there's a new fibber in town. I worked in an office full of IT geeks—people who went to sleep at night hugging their hard drives instead of their pillows. One of them said he wanted to marry a server, but at the same Christmas party I mentioned earlier (what a night that was—the entire HR department got arrested.)

I digress, sorry. Now that I thought about it, there were many prospects, but the snag was, I couldn't talk to them because I couldn't do business in my workplace! That would be highly inappropriate, and I was pretty sure it would constitute a breach of contract. The few ladies that I had enrolled from work were colleagues from a joint project with whom I was friends on FB, and they, of course, saw me drinking shakes daily.

Ah yes, I was using products in the office! Them was the days. Nobody in my upline held a corporate post, so all they could do for me was offer theoretical advice—about as helpful as sling-backs to a mermaid. I came to work to, well, work. If anyone asked what I was drinking, I could spark off a spontaneous conversation, following up with a quick message if they gave consent for me to email them.

But such curious colleagues were thin on the ground. In practice, my shake-drinking colleague did most of the talking about these shakes. Having tried every diet from Atkins to Cambridge, she was only too happy to rave about it because she saw positive results.

Why didn't I rave about my achievement? I mean, losing 20lb was no mean feat. I'm just teasing. I know precisely why I didn't climb onto the roof like a protesting prisoner, to shout my credential at the world! Objections. Unresolved, unidentified objections. More to the point, my colleague was sharing, not selling. There is a vast difference.

Score my office buddies off the prospects board, then. Great, now I'm still ten people short. And that's just on today's quota. Then I had a lightbulb moment. I know! I can update my LinkedIn profile and connect with the same people on a professional level. Sometimes I felt so sharp I had to lie down with a damp flannel over my eyes.

Chapter 8

LINKEDIN & MAXED OUT

In which: A world-weary but as yet unstoppable Peggy meets Adam, the insufferable LinkedIn guru who hits her with the hard sell — Stands amazed while $500 of her hard-earned cash leaves her account faster than a Japanese bullet train — Realises that her LinkedIn training is as valuable to her as a bicycle is to a haddock — Makes a New Year's resolution never to speak to Adam again, and keeps it!

Adam

One guy kept popping up with video tips on how to run a network marketing business on LinkedIn. He appeared to be an active associate in my company, but most of his income came from selling his expertise on how to utilise LinkedIn for your MLM business. Good for him.

Gaining proficiency on LinkedIn might allow me to connect with my office buddies. That way, at least the initial conversation could take place offsite (By the way, my corporate LinkedIn profile was in best-in-class format; I'd received specialist help during a recent redundancy, and I already had a healthy number of connections, so it made sense to try this route.)

I booked a call with Adam, the MLM LinkedIn guru, and I will not sugar coat it—I've spent more pleasurable times getting root canal treatment. I hated every minute of that conversation. He was too 'old school', obsolete in MLM preaching—sorry, Freudian slip. I meant teaching! Credit where credit is due, he was super knowledgeable about LinkedIn. But on reflection, though he only provided information already in the public domain, he made it his priority to check the small print, especially concerning LinkedIn's T&Cs. Whereas most people, including me, didn't bother creating a clever niche market for themselves.

The call was a textbook MLM scripted conversation, very similar to the 3-ways call and peeling the onion chat about your 'why'. He tried to guilt-trip me into believing he had a solution for me, and then Boom! He ended with a sales pitch. Gee whizz! Never saw that coming!

She who hesitates

And it was a sales pitch straight from Selling 101 if ever I heard one. 'Don't hesitate, Peggy. My rates go up in the New Year, but if you get the LinkedIn bundle today, you can have my one-to-one coaching for $500. I will be increasing my fees to $1000 in January because I am underselling myself for the value I can add to your business.' What a guy! Should I ask him to marry me? Nah! I was already happily married. Besides, I had enough on my plate at the moment—doing a five stretch for bigamy did not feature in my to-do list.

This conversation took place in late December. A time to deck the halls with boughs of holly. More like a time to choose between paying for the bundle or returning the kids' PlayStation and VR headset to Amazon. They'd still have a sock full of fruit and a bag of chocolate coins. Wouldn't that be enough? I mean, children get far too much nowadays, don't they?

I had been an MLM rep for a year. Indeed this was the breakthrough for which I'd yearned. I whipped out my credit card faster than John Wayne could draw his six guns. Instantly, $500 for the LinkedIn bundle whizzed out of my bank account and wafted across the Interweb, never to return. But I got him to commit to me in writing that the $500 offer for 1:1 coaching would be available to me, in the New Year, without the price increase, for showing my commitment that day.

The LinkedIn bundle contained some introductory videos on setting up my profile, which I did not need. Some advanced videos on stuff I didn't know because I had never scrutinised the T&Cs thoroughly. Pdfs, which he called 'workbooks', accompanied each video. Each pdf bore his brand logo and a big self-important blurb. Only the final page contained a useful bullet-point summary of the video's key take-aways (The jury's results are in, ladies and gentlemen: 10/10 for presentation, 5/10 for usefulness.)

Brian

Adam wasn't the kind of person with whom I would ever share a pitcher of Margarita, but he did teach me a few tricks. I researched Fiverr for a contractor who specialised in re-writing LinkedIn profiles because I wanted my new intro to be as professional as the last one. I gathered all my thoughts, highlighted key points, buzz words, and sent it over to Brian in Canada (to be accurate, he was just one of the Brians in Canada; there must have been others.) Brian was an HR recruitment professional who spent his spare time earning extra dollars contracting on Fiverr, helping clients with LinkedIn profiles, resumes and covering letters.

Brian had 100% positive feedback and many satisfied customers, so I knew I was in good hands. We exchanged many emails and collaboratively worked on re-branding my LinkedIn profile. I changed from a Business professional to a Health and Wellness Coach (it was pretty painless, actually). My intro looked as awesome as the ceiling of the Sistine Chapel. Brian had cleverly integrated my current career with my 'MLM career' to still rank on keywords for my corporate vocation, whilst I presented myself as somebody looking for clients in the Health and Wellness space. Go, Brian, go!

I made sure I turned 'Notify my network about profile changes' notifications off because I didn't want my current network to know that I had made changes—my 500+ connections connected with me because of my professional experience to date.

LinkedIn is a professional platform, and, to my mind, that is what you should use it for—not to trick people for personal gain as some do. I refuse to. I have morals.

The updates were for the new connections I planned to make because they would only ever come to know me as a 'Health and Wellness coach' (ugh), so there would be no deceitful ulterior motive to become part of my professional network.

Just for the record, Adam's advice was to present me as the 'President' or a 'CEO' of 'fill in the blanks'. He trademarked his full name as if it was a Limited company. I could not bring myself to be one of those fancy titles, so I settled for a 'Health and Wellness Coach', but I found that awkward as I was not a qualified coach. I even considered taking an online nutrition course to deserve the title!

I started to join appropriate groups and make connections. It felt much easier to click 'connect' on LinkedIn because profile displays showed only your achievements, interests, strengths and recommendations. There were no pictures of your kids, my probation officer (of course, that's a joke!) No embarrassing moments, nor people sharing inappropriate jokes with you. Thus, when somebody checked your profile, they could only read what you wanted them to read. I liked that.

I started to publish motivational posts, write articles on relevant topics concerning my products. With the benefits of the active ingredients, without ever referring to the products themselves, information on protein-pasting, adaptogens, and improving your immunity quality protein resources, you get the gist.

The LinkedIn audience was hard to please, and it was, in common with other established social media platforms—over-saturated. The objective is to build a tribe of die-hard followers, but gaining traction on LinkedIn is well known to take at least six months.

Lucy and Michael

For inspiration, I followed Lucy and Michael, reps from the UK that were killing it, on LinkedIn. They were from my neck of the woods and spoke 'my language' of brutal honesty. They stuck to the facts in a professional, non-salesy manner.

I joined some of their zoom calls on the subject of LinkedIn, too, because I was serious and determined to make this work. They were more relatable and relevant than Adam because, as fellow brits, they paid attention to severe issues like GDPR. You hardly get any sound advice from the non-Brit gurus that are super relevant to your market.

It was refreshing to hear how Lucy and Michael shared my objections to some of Adam's advice. Not sure how they came to learn about it, but they'd been around the block too many times already. They were not referring to Adam specifically but given their previous recruitment careers; they just knew what you can and cannot do on LinkedIn.

The main attraction

Above all, never title yourself as somebody you are not. Don't pretend to be somebody else if you cannot back up your claims. For example, titles like 'Body Transformation Coach', 'Visionary', 'Wealth Creation and Health Specialist', 'Holistic Wellness Coach & Online Income Creator', 'Masculinity Freedom Coach', how could you explain or prove that you were any of these things? Doesn't it sound tacky? Sorry, the last title made me throw up in my mouth, yuck! I only accepted 'Health and Wellness Coach' because I'd watched a series of online videos and read the training materials. Besides, in part justification, I was on hand 24/7. Even though I still didn't feel 100% authentic.

I don't want to sound harsh; I did get good material from Adam, just not $500' worth. But I was willing to pay the price, and he believed his time and material was worth that money. I got some great tips and a practical and straightforward daily activities checklist. I was moving forward.

I planned a week. Think of it as a to-do list. I like to-do lists. Some days I made new connections, some days I spent endorsing people, other days I would post an article that I would share on other social platforms, which would result in directing people back to my LinkedIn profile. I started group discussions and performed searches with keywords relevant to my current career to connect with similar people. I reckoned that if I was interested in this business and earning extra cash, there had to be similar people in my network in the same boat (Soon to be re-launched as the SS Success.)

It makes sense, right? Look on LinkedIn now and type into the search bar any MLM company that springs to mind, filter by people, and you will see how many ordinary folks with regular jobs are also involved in MLM.

On accepting your connection requests, you introduce yourself and welcome them to your network via private message. This was the part I struggled with because the templates and the scripted spiel did not sound like me. Adam was American, and their market was different to the UK market. We talked to people differently.

That's why I was so excited to find Lucy and Michael because they lived in my region! So I used their templates with a bit of personalisation. I started counting the noes like I was supposed to, getting excited because each one edged me closer to that elusive yes.

I never got as far as scheduling the first phone call with a prospect to test the later templates from Adam. They ignored my messages. Or I received the LinkedIn prefilled reply or was politely rejected. But I continued to follow the daily checklist because I wanted to be consistent. Besides, I very much agreed with these steps to grow your professional network. I noticed that more people started requesting me to join their network. They were looking to expand their network, and the buzzwords in my profile fitted their filter criteria. This began to feel like traction, at last.

As soon as I accepted, I received a private message to thank me and welcome me to their network and look at their opportunity or sell me their course because they were mainly coaches helping their clients grow their network or acquire more customers. I never ignored any of the messages; I politely turned them around and said, 'Welcome to my network' before graciously declining their offer. Strange feeling to be hounded, to experience the shoe on the other foot.

This was when I paused to consider whether this side hustle was for me after all. As a network marketer, I knew that I must grow skin as thick as that on a rhino's butt so that I could step outside of my comfort zone. But that was a place I remained loathe to visit.

I continued to use LinkedIn, and to this day, I still follow some of my daily tasks from back then. We should all support our network, and it costs nothing to endorse somebody who has impacted you or recommend them if they are looking for the next opportunity.

I always comment on people's work anniversaries and keep in touch with those small likes. These are small gestures, but it keeps the algorithm happy, and maybe it enhances their chances of getting the job of their dreams.

You probably think that I failed LinkedIn because I couldn't follow instructions. Not for the first time, I wasn't prepared to put myself in an uncomfortable situation that compromised my sense of morality. And before you start saying that successful MLM folks have morals and integrity, too, hear me out. We are all made from different dough, and they are prepared to go all in and put their name 100% behind the company. Whereas I was not prepared to be Peggy X, aka The Shake Lady. That was not my lifelong ambition. There was absolutely nothing wrong with it, but I had different plans for my brand. My original objective was to make money to support my other business's purchase of a quality inventory to make an impact, and hopefully a tiny fortune, elsewhere.

It came down to this: did I have the necessary burning desire—that fire in the belly? Unfortunately, no matter how long I'd been rubbing two sticks together like a conscientious Girl Scout, I may have occasionally smouldered, but never once did I burst across the heavens like a Magic Kingdom fireworks display at Disneyland. Hence LinkedIn never brought any prospects to my downline. And in case you are wondering, I've not spoken to Adam ever again.

Chapter 9

FORGET JURASSIC PARK – WELCOME TO MLM WORLD

In which: Peggy reinvents herself as a Health and Wellness Coach — Feels the joy of home tasting parties — Becomes dazzled looking at before and after photos — Accepts as collateral damage, the loss of two rainforests and a small wood in her drive to print a mountain of publicity leaflets — Amber the Abacus rides to the rescue!

The problem with ruthlessly applying the adage, 'don't reinvent the wheel!' Is that, from an IT perspective, you never see the need to upgrade from the system your Uncle Frank gave you as a graduation gift in 1996: The IBM with the 4-inch green screen and the floppy disk. You couldn't give this stuff away at a car-boot sale now.

The kit in MLM World was as dated as a lava lamp. The kind of kit that, had it been a shop window mannequin, would have been wearing a kipper tie and bell-bottomed trousers. Okay, that may sound a little ungrateful considering the company tried to give us great tools and fancy apps, but the content and style were a bit home knitted for my taste.

Let me show you what I mean. Let's take a peek at the life of a Health and Wellness coach.

There were too many MLM companies on the market then. Many still bogged down in thinking MLM was a pyramid scheme, and if you did not innovate your methods, you were not winning. That's not true. A fraction of the reps were winning, but not everybody. Those who came on board a decade earlier were winning. It was the new kids on the block that couldn't get traction.

It's my party, and I'll cry if I want to

I organised home tasting parties, inviting people through private messaging, creating curiosity on FB, making it sound like the best party since Glastonbury. Missing it would leave refuseniks with a case of FOMO fit to depress them for a month.

I rustled up protein balls, macheted protein chocolate bars into nibble-sized pieces, served some mango and papaya juice and lashings of Prosecco. I arranged 'before' and' after' pictures of real product users across the table. I scattered some leaflets and brochures and primed an intro video on my laptop.

I think I became a trifle unhinged, ordering grandiose amounts of stationery, including a massive banner, business cards, leaflets with my contact information. I printed a stack of product information and price lists. Then I had an attack of stupid and laminated them all, rendering every single sheet useless the first time the prices changed.

I laminated 'before' and 'after' pictures, you name it; I bought it because I thought that way lay success. Whatever merchandise I could get my hands on, I purchased. I even bought a whiteboard to draw the compensation plan in front of my 'live' audience. If my party looked professional, I would look competent and qualified to talk about this opportunity, and people would be jumping at the chance to join my bandwagon.

Unfortunately, the 'optics' was a bit wonky. Potential candidates thinking of signing with me would focus on the extravagance of my party preparations and start fretting about their potential up-front costs. Regrettably, I was too busy at the time, willing the laminator to work faster (the laminator is the world's most annoyingly slow gadget).

Ask me how many people came to my parties. 'C'mon... I dare you!' I'll give you a clue; the answer is singular. One! One frickin' person!

I planned a party every three weeks. Advertising, inviting friends that said they had plans last time but would come next time. Some said yes, and never turned up; some excused themselves an hour before the party claiming loved ones had suddenly come down with beriberi or Dengue fever, but maybe next time, eh?

They often ignored my messages. I soothed myself that these people were misguided fools, missing out on this great opportunity! I knew this happened to everybody, even to the millionaire leaders. They'd had more empty rooms than a derelict Salvation Army Citadel. My positivity glands were working at warp factor six—if nobody at all turned up, I'd reframe the evening as a 'mock' party—a practice run. It was all grist for the mill.

Typically you invited your upline for support and your teammates to give you testimonials. Still, since I was the current holder of the company's prestigious Betty-No -Mates shield, I ran the show on my own with help from my enthusiastic 10-year-old.

Okay, go ahead and laugh if you must. You have my permission. There was no show; nobody ever turned up except for that one person, that one time. I did my best to follow the protocol, but nerves got the better of me, and I was all over the place. She made cooing sounds over the protein balls and admitted she'd been to a similar party before. That perked me up, but she made it clear from the start she was just nosey and had no intentions of joining me as a customer or a rep.

Did I run and hide in the airing cupboard with a bottle of Asti Spumante? Not at all. Once I realised I had nothing to sell this woman, all tension left me. I experienced a twinge of emotional pain when I saw her the next day on the school grounds. To this day, we are still friends. Phew!

An experienced leader advised me to take photos of my party and create a FOMO amongst the back-stabbing bastards, those with legitimate reasons for failing to show on the night. Besides, these soirées were tax-deductible, so you can put the products you prepared and consumed during the party, including the Prosecco, on your tax returns. I was to keep my receipts and date my photos to forward them to my accountant at the end of the tax year.

My accountant—Amber, the Abacus, could shake all your numbers like snow in a snow globe, and they'd all settle back down in exactly the right place. I'm just not sure she ever thought of inviting me over to her home for cheese and wine to celebrate our sisterhood. I base her stand-offishness on the comments she made when I sent her photographic evidence of my sparsely attended introduction party.

AMBER THE ABACUS: ...and these are the snaps taken at your party?

ME: Yes!

AMBER THE ABACUS: So why did you go on PhotoShop to airbrush out all your guests?

ME: I didn't!

AMBER THE ABACUS: but—that would mean nobody turned up.

ME: No one did

AMBER THE ABACUS: Not a party at all, then?

ME: S'pose not.

As you can imagine, the only FOMO I created was of my beautiful table full of goodies and merchandise. Still, I wasn't allowed to directly show my company's logo or give away the names of my products, so I had to get good at taking photos at an angle that showed next to nothing worth seeing. I don't know why we didn't take the photographs with the lights off and the curtains closed. The idea was to demonstrate how epic tonight was going to be. So much so that your street cred would take a nosedive were you to miss the next party in three weeks.

Here again, was the same half-baked logic I'd railed against previously. They expected us to be proud of what we promoted, but we could not talk about it directly on social media. I suspected that this rule had been ring-fenced exclusively for us, the wannabe millionaires, aka the future failed network marketers, because none of the millionaire leaders seemed shy in this regard. I suppose you could say they'd earned the bragging rights.

There were no 'party' pictures because it would end up being a selfie with my beautiful display, and I was not that sad. Associates with a successful party full of participants would often take a gazillion pictures (half a gazillion on slow nights) to show off. Some associates who did not have any new participants but were joined by their teammates would post photos of themselves—the same crowd every time, but at least it was a crowd. I felt a tad jealous, so I Googled 'crowd' for a definition. The wording didn't rule out the possibility of the one person who turned up to my party being a crowd, but neither did it rule it in. Maybe if she'd moved about a lot more? So, an inconclusive result.

Leaflets

Loggers hacked down swathes of forest to create the paper for the thousands of leaflets I purchased, which contained details of my epic opportunity. My kids helped me distribute these throughout our town.

We all know the life-cycle of the common or garden leaflet ends tragically at the recycle bin. But you never know (there's that optimism again) there might be somebody desperately searching for the solution I offered. It was worth a shot.

I conducted an MLM Leaflet Distribution boot camp for the kids, mainly to prevent my arrest, if I'm honest. I mean, they were too young to go to prison, but I wasn't.

I concentrated on teaching them how to walk briskly away from signs that said,

- ☐ No Junk mail
- ☐ No leaflets
- ☐ No Cold Callers
- ☐ Salespeople shove off
- ☐ Warning, Dobermann Pinschers
- ☐ Single, double or treble glazing salespeople should jog right along.
- ☐ Warning to uninvited callers: I don't know who you are. I don't know what you want. If you are looking for ransom, I can tell you I don't have money. But what I do have is a very particular set of skills, skills I have acquired over a very long career. Skills that make me a nightmare for people like you. If you take your opportunity leaflets elsewhere, that'll be the end of it. I will not look for you; I will not pursue you. But if you don't, I will look for you, I will find you, and I will kill you.

I especially stressed this last bullet point because I could see them in my mind's eye, robotically stuffing these leaflets through every letterbox in the postal district as a zookeeper might feed fish to penguins. They'd each be desperate to get rid of their armful of paper before their sibling. Perhaps I overstressed these rules, but the last thing I wanted was to get reported to the police, and because they had to be, my full name and mobile number were on those leaflets! They wouldn't need Sherlock and Watson to track me down.

I bought a wheelbarrow load of business cards, printed with a logo I'd commissioned from a designer, and which looked like a replica of the official seal of the Austrian-Hungarian Empire.

I intended to always carry a bunch of business cards with me for handing them to prospects. I'd been taught that the alternative to getting people's contact details was to open my FB page in the search bar and ask them to find themselves and send them a friend request. Ugh! Really? I never got the vibe that these strangers wanted to be my FB friends. Business cards seemed more straightforward, although I must agree, the downside was that I empowered others to connect with me. They, of course, walked away, counting their blessings that they got rid of me and setting a New Year's resolution, regardless of the actual date, never to speak to me again. Whereas, if I had their details, I could always send a friendly follow up.

I distributed some of my business cards at local supermarket advertising sections, local hair and beauty salons. It remains one of the universe's mysteries. However, I am still waiting for the first candidate, someone who wants to improve their sleep or ease their anxiety, ring a person they have never met, and offer protein shakes as a solution.

Sigh

Stalls

Not to worry. I got a bit of traction at the school Christmas and Easter markets and at the local quarterly Artisan market, where budding entrepreneurs attempted to sell hats made from twigs or marmalade-and-quinoa-flavoured toffee apples.

I went all in-Texas Hold 'em style. I bought a tablespace for fifteen quid, laid out my tablecloth, carefully arranged all my products, including the blender, shaker, small shot glasses for sampling the drinks, more protein balls with a big fat 'contains nuts' warning sign, lots of other goodies, brochures, before and after pictures, my humongous stand, a little quiz and spare pens.

My kids often accompanied me. They thought it exciting to have their mum at school 'selling' something. They felt they had purpose instead of just hovering around other people's stalls like moths around a flame until packing-up time.

The wonders of the Empire weren't on offer here. The scale was more petite. If you went around once, you'd see it all; school halls are pretty tiny. At least with their mum having a stall, the kids felt like they had a base, and when one friend left, the next friend arrived, so they were always occupied. I have set up stalls in my kids' school and other schools around our town, but it was usually the same stalls, same faces, same stuff.

Some people have made a career out of these markets, and you got to meet talented craftspeople who could carve tableaux from the Siege of Stalingrad out of a slab of Cheddar cheese and many other MLM reps pushing their products.

Nobody offered what I offered, which was nice. Nobody else had stationery bearing the royal seal of the Austro-Hungarian Empire, which was also lovely. I stood out. Yet hardly anybody stopped by my table. I watched people from the moment they walked in. They'd scan the room, find the stall that appeared to be selling some marzipan tidbits, with sample pieces already cut up. But as they passed my booth, they magically gained velocity and sped by (had someone left a door open? October gales couldn't have blown them—it was still the middle of May.) On the rare occasion when people bothered to stop, it was almost always for the free food.

The nice thing about these markets was the friendliness of the fellow stall sellers—the prisoner of war camp camaraderie. I liked to talk to the MLM consultants because I was curious to know what they thought of their products, how well they were selling and how they found their company. It seemed I was the only 'part-timer'. Everyone else focused on this full-time and made a living out of it.

You could sense their passion for their company and products. This was a game in which they commanded the pitch. It was evident they were in it to win it. Their livelihoods depended on it.

One lady at a Christmas market did her best to sell craft scarfs fashioned from dandelion leaves stained by dye derived from crushed lupins. She was back to back with me. We became overly friendly after one too many glasses of mulled wine, and we had a good laugh. She introduced me to lucrative markets that I knew existed, but it never occurred to me as a potential event in which I could take part.

Corporate stalls! Why didn't I think of that! I had been to a few myself, my corporate organisation hosted them regularly, and I even bought some stuff there. Now that would have been perfect! They were consistently popular with the staff, and considering the company I work for had many buildings and sites; it would have been ideal.

The only snag was, I was not a permanent employee but an external resource, and if I took time off, I did not get paid. Would it have been worth it? Probably not. Would they allow me to do it anyway regardless of my status, permie or contractor?

Corporate advertising

I remember asking one of the Sodexo guys on our floor to distribute my leaflets throughout all the breakout areas, and he kindly offered to do it for me. There were leaflets everywhere you looked, obviously nothing as irrelevant as protein shakes, but I thought it would be okay with their permission. Wrong!

While working from home, I got a Skype message from one of the company directors, asking me if those leaflets were mine. Somebody must have dobbed me in. Where was I? Communist China? My heart was in my throat; I genuinely thought I would be hung, drawn and quartered.

I explained that I had done so with the permission of the facility management team, who distributed it on my behalf. 'Anyone in particular?' She asked, four nanoseconds before I threw him under the bus with full disclosure of his name, rank and serial number (at least the corporate equivalent.)

Great! Was the company about to celebrate a double sacking? As it turned out, they slapped my wrists, but we hung on to our jobs. As a bonus, they allowed me to leave a single leaflet in one of the kitchen areas. Phew! What a lucky escape.

I could target other corporate companies, but was I willing to sacrifice my daily rate plus travel? Um, no. Corporate stalls sounded lucrative but turned out to be wholly impractical in my case. But I would highly recommend it to anybody serious or in a full-time network marketing business.

Gyms

Gyms were also a fabulous place to acquire customers. But if you could enlist a gym owner, you might have hit the jackpot. Think about CrossFit, for example, or a personal trainer! I dare you to dream with me! Imagine enticing a PT who believed in your products 100%, and you placed them in your downline. Oh yeah! The number of people he could introduce into your organisation was compelling. This could have been the deal-breaker for you! From wannabe associate to successful biz builder! Overnight! Well, maybe not that fast.

There was nothing more frustrating for a PT than having a client who worked their ass off one hour a week when under their watch but was not getting results. They would soon think that they were wasting money and quit. But if they could control what their clients put in their mouth when they were not with them, they would soon start to see results and recommend the PT to their friends. It was all about word of mouth advertising, the most effective way to get recommendations.

One of our leaders was highly skilled in attaining business through gyms! She did a FB live video about the steps she took to approach gym owners and kindly answered everybody's burning questions. She was one of the millionaire leaders with her fancy website. This was when I wished I'd signed up under somebody like her or was somewhere in her organisation downline. She was a proper credit to the company and lived by the motto, 'one team'. She was approachable and thrilled to answer my private messages with my endless queries and doubts. Definitively a graceful leader to stalk on Facebook and Instagram because I could learn from her.

Global presence

As a network marketer, I knew there were many ways to attract new customers. Face to face, or as some old-school MLM professionals call it, belly to belly. Never limit yourself to people in your workplace only, friends, family, and neighbours. There are billions of people on this earth; one should never run out of people to talk to.

My favourite trainer, another one I secretly wished to be part of his downline, lived in Australia. He often travelled to speak at our UK events. He was uber-funny and relatable. And he did not do anything by half. He and his wife got to millionaire status in record-breaking time. His motto was 'unstoppable'. When my company opened up in the UK market, he gave us all a speech in which he proclaimed that if we did not get to work, he would move his family to the UK and prune the place. A year later, he did move to England, and surprise surprise, he was the number 1 UK income earner.

If your company is global, you can have teams in all the markets where your company has a presence. You can imagine how happy his UK team was to have him on British soil. Luckily, we all benefited from his wisdom; he was active in the company Facebook groups, sharing tips, motivating us, and freely giving us his templates. Another sophisticated leader added to my 'stalk/follow' list.

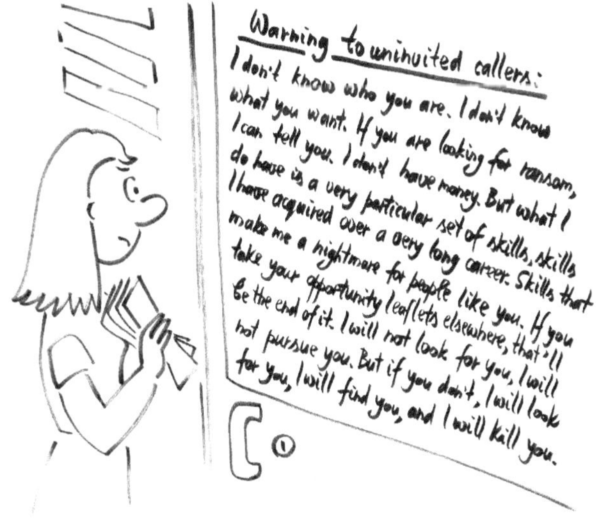

Chapter 10

SOCIAL MEDIA – THE BASICS (WELL, I AM OVER 40, YOU KNOW.)

In which: Peggy gives up privacy — struggles to grow a rhino hide — Gets baffled by the black arts of social media algorithms — Resolves to conquer the digital world, one platform at a time — Discovers that the Beatles were wrong when they said 'All you need is love.' The MLM version is better: 'All you need is WiFi.'

The modern way to build a network marketing business is online. They'd sell you, 'Build your financial freedom from your phone— all you need is WiFi'.

Easy-Peasy, right? Indeed only a buffoon would not have a smartphone in the 21st century, huh? Our whole life history was on the bloody phone! Most of us had social media, and if we didn't, you just created a new account for free. It just depended on which particular social platform you were comfortable with, or in my case, I understood the most. They each served a different purpose, followed other principles, but whatever social media I chose, I had to be prepared to lose my privacy and make sure I grew that rhino butt skin.

Twitter

I never understood Twitter. Or tweeting. Nor what good it could do me. So I never created a personal account for MLM bragging. The only Twitter account I had was for my failed product I mentioned at the beginning. But I was rubbish at maintaining it and engaging with the audience.

Instagram

Instagram seemed popular with MLM guys. They all boasted beautiful pictures, visual representations of their financial freedom, creating FOMO, looking like celebrities with tons of money, and travelling the globe.

I wasn't a fan, but I danced the bandwagon tango just the same because I watched a training video from a leader killing it through IG. Thousands of followers joined her each week, and I wanted a slice of that pie.

Was this the missing link to my success? You needed to set up your business for IG, so it was 'open' for people to follow you without your permission. To make Instagram work for you, you had to find a unique hashtag that could represent your brand and use it consistently with your pictures and utilise all the allowed up to 30 hashtags for your image.

If you had enticing, high-quality content to go with your picture, you improved your chances significantly of being viewed by the largest audience. I am sure you've noticed that people who do well on Instagram almost always have professional looking magazine-ready photos.

They use some alternate photos with quotes so that their home page has a tidy pattern. They choose one or two dominant colours and use them consistently. This gives rise to classy-looking profiles that sharply represent their brand. They use IG stories to promote their products, talk directly to their audience, do little competitions, share their thoughts, have a little cry to show their raw emotional side or just rant. They are ninja masters at it.

I promised myself I'd post daily, mirroring what my idols did, and aimed my page at the fitness enthusiast. So I posted my pre-workout and post-workout juices and supplements from the gym. I posted motivational messages to inspire my small following to plug their mojo back into the mains, get up off their arses and do some good with their lives. The only problem was, I had not won any Pussycat Doll lookee-likee contests lately (by which I mean never). I did not look lush in leggings. Nor was the aptest adjective you might use to describe my makeup, 'flawless'. Even the pick of my photos bore an uncanny resemblance to Sweaty Betty's twin sister, Greasy Gertrude.

Not a pretty sight! But a few random people started following me, though that was thanks to the hashtags, not my good looks. However, what I did not know at the time was that bots operated IG. Depending on hashtags, you got a 'like' or a 'follow'. But by the evening, those followers disappeared. I never studied it intensely, but behind every social media, lay a strategy, logic and algorithm that would have been exhausting to learn.

I put my best foot forward. I posted to IG, hooked up my FB account and therefore posted to both platforms with a single click. Winner! To satisfy your curiosity, I never gained a single prospect through IG. I got hounded by others to view their products or opportunities and some inappropriate messages I chose to report and delete.

Facebook

And finally, everybody's chum and pal—good old Facebook. I already had a private FB account with friends and family I interacted with daily. If you had friends from around the globe like me that you hadn't spoken to in ages, it was nice to stroll down memory lane together.

Gems like your failed cake attempts or a joke, or the time you tasered the gardener by mistake. If denied the luxury of seeing everybody regularly, this was the next best thing. I have had a FB account since 2007; I even remember who invited me to join! It was so exciting to try to find your long-lost friends and spy on your ex-boyfriends, who they had married and if they had kids.

I duly turned my privacy off, so the world and his wife could see my morning shake photos, my sweat-lathered face and all the educational posts and photos of my products (without the name of the product, of course—that would never do). I hated knowing everybody could see what I did on my page; I felt exposed as if every day was my first day at a nudist colony. But remember, they said I must step outside my comfort zone and deliberately make myself vulnerable; hence I felt I had no choice.

Sigh

When I thought about it, there were plenty of things I could do that would catapult me so far outside my comfort zone I'd need to take a taxi back. Here's three to be going on with:

- ☐ Accompanying my mother to her over-sixties twerking club, so I could hold her Zimmer when it was her turn on stage during competitions.
- ☐ Enrolling in a naked limbo dancing course run by the local council, in which the only other members were middle-aged male accountants with comb-overs, a permanent leer, and beer bellies that made

them look like they had stuffed a 16-pound bowling ball up their faded tank-tops.

- ☐ Participation in any form of bog-snorkelling.

The top three unofficial rules for posting on social media were 'be positive', 'be positive' and, yes, you've guessed it, 'be positive'. Never project any negative vibes—of the sort you might radiate were you to become stuck in a lift with nobody to talk to until the fire brigade arrived, but Roy Keane and Pearce Morgan. Never post political views, especially your own. Don't engage in arguments.

If you got a horrible comment, simply 'Bless, release, and delete'—post at least five times a day, family, day-to-day stuff and then one power post. A power post might concern the impact your products had on you or before-and-after results. Anything relating to what the extra income meant for you and your family always worked well too.

When you power-posted, you immediately asked for support from your teammates to appease the beast that was the FB algorithm. The aim is for your post to appear on top of your friend's wall. The more engagement you get, the better your visibility. If it were immediately after it has been posted, FB would consider you to be an influencer as famous as a Mr Whippy ice-cream van during a heatwave and show more of your stuff.

Each team had some form of messenger group where you would announce that you had just posted and would appreciate the support. You scratch my back, and I'll scratch yours. Don't come asking for help if you are not willing to help others, so often people would say 'please comment on my post, I'm going to your wall now' because they've not really been proactive and only become active when in need, they remembered to reciprocate.

You could also join a group for anybody from our MLM company. You specifically asked reps from around the globe to contribute with comments, too, in the forlorn hope that they'll find a reason to bother doing so instead of washing their hair, changing their socks, or shaving their legs.

This was one reason your profile needed to be public; otherwise, random strangers could not comment. Unfortunately, you have as much control over random strangers as you do the weather. The risk of fielding super-cringy comments that gave away the fact that they were fellow MLM sales-hungry people was high.

I used this group as sparingly as a down-market cafe used natural beef in their Chilli con Carne because some people would get little traction from their power posts, and as soon as I asked for help, they would jump at the chance and leave a cringe-worthy comment on my post. Then they came back to my original post in that group, commented 'done, now mine'.

As you can see, people had a legitimate reason to avoid commenting in the first place. Now you were forced to reciprocate on a post with which you disagreed. Maybe you genuinely didn't know what to say yet still felt compelled to do it.

Cringe

TikTok

I recently watched a video by a super successful MLM coach who tipped TikTok as the platform destined to become the most significant thing since Boots the Chemist loaded their shelves with Philips Lady Shavers. Both of my kids have a TikTok account— they dance during dinner whilst brushing their teeth. It seems like they cannot talk to me nowadays without jiggling or body-popping.

I'm not even going to investigate it, but if you're still convinced you can make it as a network marketing rep, my advice is to gain a good following. However, between writing, editing and publishing this book, TikTok became the first social networking platform to ban content promoting pyramid schemes and multi-level marketing companies.

The social media network updated community guidelines in December 2020 to ask users not to post or share content that 'depicts or promotes Ponzi, multi-level marketing, or pyramid schemes.' Their latest guidelines read, 'We do not permit anyone to exploit our platform to take advantage of users' trust and bring about financial or personal harm.' So if you do go on TikTok, be sure not to promote your MLM.

Bummer! What if other social networking platforms follow suit? Wow, you are done! Your biz is gone! Your work from home, work from your phone, laptop lifestyle is gone! It's back to preying on village people in the supermarket again.

To this day, I have come closer to unravelling Fermat's last theorem than I have to decipher a single social media algorithm. I know as much about these platforms as I do about the Suez Crisis of 1956. There are plenty of people out there earning a living out of understanding the black magic underpinnings of social media and claiming guru status. Trust me, if you stopped to blow your nose when they were passing by, they'd try to sell you a course.

I think nobody will ever be up to date with it. What's essential to recognise is don't try to grasp all platforms at once. Focus on a single platform. Read T&Cs, watch videos from the source, learn from YouTube, observe what successful people in any network marketing do on that platform. Watch and learn.

Nothing prevents you from following people from another organisation (I would not recommend befriending them on FB, though). You could build a good following and take it from there. Try to have a presence on too many social platforms at once, and you will never understand how any of them work. Master one, to a reasonable degree and by all means, spread your wings.

Chapter 11

EARN WHILE YOU LEARN

In which: Peggy considers the validity of 'earn while you learn' - gets miffed with double standards - reconsiders whether she is coachable — Mind is everything, everything is mind. - discovers the Holy Grail of personal development.

The best part about MLM was personal development. The way they sold this business was you 'earn while you learn'. Fair point. Which other company allowed you to do that? Well, not brain surgery and Rocket Science for a start.

At a more mundane level, being a dental surgeon doesn't quite fit the bill either.

DENTAL STUDENT: It's a great course. I earn while I learn. Last week I left a patient's teeth in but removed their gums by mistake! I still got fifty quid. And I'll know better next time.

You had to lay out capital upfront for most traditional businesses, and you had to be a specialist in your chosen field. Nine out of ten times, you had to ask for a loan, and who was going to lend you money if you said, 'I will learn my trade as I go'? No one.

TRAINEE HIGH-SPEED RAIL TRAIN DRIVER: Four hundred pounds a week plus a non-contributory pension and a free daily corned beef sandwich from the buffet car worth £8.40? I'll have some of that!

CRITIC: But what if you take a 40 mph bend at 160 mph, derailing the train and killing 50 people.

TRAINEE HIGH-SPEED RAIL TRAIN DRIVER: I'll take the bend slower the next time. Are you saying I'd have to pay for the sandwich?

Double standards

I agreed with the 'earn whilst you learn' statement when I first started. I still agreed with it and believed it at my first event. Still, as my credit card bill expanded faster than the known universe and with the sheer volume of information you needed to stay on top of getting larger by the day, my head was ready to lift off from my shoulders and hurtle into a low Earth orbit.

I followed my upline's advice to the letter, but I was miffed when I saw others doing the exact opposite. Double standards! For example, I was slapped hard round the chops, given a Chinese burn on my left shin and scowled at continuously for ten minutes for commenting on somebody's post, partially using the company's name. It was not enough to decipher it if you asked me. One of the leaders reported it on their 'leader' messenger group.

They immediately identified my upline, who asked me to amend it. I over-reacted, feeling like the police had caught me red-handed stealing bread from the kitchen of an orphan's home. Would they insist on a custodial sentence? I hung my head so low in shame that I started banging into lamp posts.

I instantly updated my comment removing the offending word and feeling like a village idiot's stupider sister for being told off. But then my mood shifted to frustration and a full-blown persecution complex. Why was I not contacted directly? Why was I made to feel like a scullery maid who had shoddily polished the silver?

As I said previously, it was verboten to upload to Social Media an image of the whole product or its name. We had to use emojis to cover up the names. Or take a photo from such an unnatural angle; nobody could see what it was. It would end up looking like one of those puzzle photographs they used to print in magazines, of everyday objects shot from strange angles, and you had to guess what the thing was. Like a toilet brush snapped from Earth orbit.

A photograph of a toilet brush shot from Earth orbit was unlikely to add value to my campaign, so I didn't bother. But then you'd visit somebody else's wall to see everything in view, with no effort whatsoever made to hide any part of it! It made the hairs in my armpits stand to attention in mute protest.

I used to screenshot offenders' sites and send the image to my upline. She'd say, 'It's a recommendation because you are trying to create curiosity, and yeah, some reps do that'.

What the heck? That made me try to grip the carpet with my toes through my trainers.

Anyway, you live and learn and follow the group's rules, because you must be coachable, because only coachable people make it in this biz, right?

Learning and personal development

As I learnt about my company and products, I discovered more about network marketing. There were hundreds of books on MLM, thousands of YouTube videos. Where should I start? Luckily, my upline shared some incredible, company-approved Vimeos specific to my company. We can all learn from successful leaders.

There were more recordings of live training, interviews, and podcasts than David Attenborough had made monkey movies. We are all different and relate to other people, so it was best to find that one successful leader (or leaders) you'd made a connection with the most and focus on their material.

That's what I did. I followed a few favourite couples. No disrespect to my team and upline, but they were not my kind of people. I mean, none had horns on their head or anything like that, I would gladly share a pitcher of Margarita with them, but I wouldn't choose them as business partners.

Following others was recommended because not everybody invited to do business had an upline that could teach them or was interested in building MLM business themselves. You could be 4 or 5 layers deep from somebody who was doing this business—which meant you were probably nearer to being next in line for the Queen of England's job than you were to them, but who says they idolise you?

I would compare it to family. You cannot choose them the way you choose your friends, but that doesn't mean you have to like them.

I met an Uber-smart dude at one event. He wanted to join our company but did not know any reps, so he went straight to the top. He contacted the owners directly. They put him in touch with a highly successful couple who had been trainers in many of our events. Being mentored by the best saw his business booming just two months in.

He spent much of his time hoovering up the bonuses available to those who strapped into the helm of the Starship MLM and built their business at warp factor six. I often wished I could change teams, but I would be naïve to think that I could do any better if I had a successful and dedicated upline.

A little bit yin, a little bit yang

It was all about mindset. And this is where my story gets a bit cosmic, a tad Hare Krishna. So you might want to slip on your favourite tie-dye headband and that pair of saffron-coloured pantaloons you haven't worn since college. Now breath in through the soles of your feet. Good. And out through the top of your head, and listen up.

Gautama Buddha said it all when he said, 'Mind is everything. What you think you become.' How true. No amount of influence would make me successful if I weren't convinced. I thought my mind was in the right place. My biggest obstacles were my unresolved objections, so I worked on those, though they were as hard to pin down as stuffing a live eel into a jam-jar with your bare hands.

Personal development is super important in every aspect of your life; besides, I love to learn. Funny how we hate learning when we are at school—no S3 student ever faints with excitement on their way to a trigonometry lesson and has to be revived with smelling salts. But step outside the school, and we develop an unshakeable thirst for knowledge. Or is it just me?

After being made redundant a few years before being introduced to Network Marketing, I started my development journey. Those with more wisdom than I ever had said that the trip of a thousand miles begins with one step. I get that; I'm cool with the first step; you just have to put one foot in front of another. It's the thought of the sixty million steps that come after the first step that gave me the colly-wobbles.

I had an excellent job with a reputable company, but they were moving most departments to a different part of the UK. I assumed they were doing so for sound business reasons and not out of mischief. Anyway, they decided to re-locate everyone (who still had a job) to a purpose-built site and our existing site sold.

Furthermore, they were outsourcing more and more jobs to third parties, so we had a wave of redundancies. I put my best foot forward (remember the journey of a thousand miles) and threw my hat in the ring for redundancy because although I liked my job, it had become as stimulating as watching a silent movie with a blindfold on.

Besides, only someone whose head zipped up the back would quit voluntarily if there was the slightest possibility of securing a severance package. So, I was excited to see what the future might hold. Naturally, I felt scared at the same time because it was a cushy job that paid above the market rate. Those jobs are rarer than unicorn poop.

But I was 37, and on reflection, I thought this would be a perfect opportunity to make a fresh start. I could finally awaken the slumbering entrepreneur (might 'currently comatose entrepreneur' be a more accurate description?) within me and eventually be my own boss.

The wheels of the company's redundancy processing machine turned slowly in contrast with that of others who were quite capable of telling you not to bother coming in the following Monday. For decades, many of us had worked for the company, 11 years in my case, in our little global bubble of 60,000 employees—a unique self-sustaining ecosystem. We understood that we might feel dysfunctional in the outside world.

I often compared my work environment to my husband's and was often dismayed by how poorly regulated his workplace was. A lack of procedures, strategies as ill-defined as a politician's pledges. Worst of all, they had little regard for individual needs.

That said, the difference between working in a global IT company compared to a small scale outfit was massive. Multinational companies have separate departments for each IT component. Whereas many small IT teams consisted of a spotty Herbert called Colin, with an eight terabyte hard drive and a goatee beard. Across the land, a small army of Colins handled everything from system reboots to glueing the arm back on your workstation chair when it falls off.

We would soon have to steel ourselves for life outside the gates of our corporate citadel, out there in the natural, scary world.

Redundancy machine

The company allocated each redundancy candidate a bag of jelly babies and a certain number of points to spend on their most wanted training. Or on one-to-one workshopping with a world-class HR organisation that focused on the employment lifecycle, including career transition (Confession: I lied about the jelly babies! But that's because the process of redundancy is as colourless as the drapes in a funeral parlour. I hope you will forgive me.)

I was already running on the spot three months before my termination, planning my transition like a military campaign, booking the right consultants in advance, making sure I had enough points to cover everything I needed. Other sessions were points' free' such as consultation with the JobCentre Plus, planning for retirement, and others.

If I could have attended two sessions in different locations simultaneously, I would have, but I suspected that this was beyond the capabilities of Doctor Who. I liked that many of the consultants were the presenters of sessions that only cost a few points, but at least you got an introduction. Once you'd gone through all the sessions, you had to decide which coach would be the most suitable for the 1:1 deep dive session.

This was when I created my first LinkedIn profile, sculpting it under expert guidance into a work of art that would have made Michaelangelo jealous. Another specialist—a true wordsmith—crafted my CV beautifully. I learnt to distinguish between a Limited company and a Limited Partnership. I gained unlimited access to the HR career transition company resource's website. I received valuable hand-outs and felt robustly supported. I had never been through this before, and I felt like a child learning to ride her first bike, but a bike to which the company had attached pretty good stabiliser wheels.

All this support was available during working hours, and you could have knocked me over with a feather duster when I heard that some of my colleagues failed to take advantage of these sessions. Too busy! With what? Clearing their desks? Doing the last of the filing?

They were leaving their job, the company was offering to help them transition to the real world, yet they could not find the time to attend? Madder than a shoebox of frogs! I raved about this service. I gave feedback on every meeting I attended and told anybody who'd listen (including passers-by) about this fantastic opportunity. You could not get this kind of service anywhere on the open market unless you mortgaged your house to finance it.

This was when I got my first delicious taste for personal development and realised there was more to life than the slim pickings offered by the daily grind.

One of the sessions was with Life Coaches. I had never heard of them. Of course, they probably explained this to us during their introduction, but I still did not have a clue.

All I remember is that they allowed us to dream and draw a picture of where we saw ourselves in 5 years. I liked this. I liked this a lot. It was not something I'd ever done before, because my life had long been the typical hamster wheel of bare existence: Let the dog drag you around the local park before the sun came up, negotiate the school run (which had elements of the Belgian Grand Prix), work, grab a meal deal, including a bag of Pickled Onion Monster Munch and a tin of full-fat Coke, work again, sleep, repeat. I never imagined that this was a prison yard from which anyone might escape because bills constantly stamp their feet, demanding your attention like a two-year-old, and work was the only way to appease them.

Plus, I was privileged to work for a respectable employer, so why would I want to rattle the boat? (Or is it 'rock the cage?' I forget.) If you have an entrepreneurial spirit, it could be a disadvantage to work for a decent employer.

Should you have become unhinged enough to resign, your spouse, family, friends, acquaintances from Weight Watchers, and possibly even the headmaster of your last school might smile benignly at you at first. Still, when that wears off, they'd have a whip-round to fund the hire of a carpenter and a flatbed truck. With everyone on board, they run you up to the top of the nearest hill and crucify you to a makeshift cross with decking screws (nails are sooo yesterday in the modern world of joinery), especially if you had young children.

Working for a crappy little company that treated their minions like...well, minions, was a different story. It almost spurred you into action, and you could justify choosing to leave to experiment with a different life.

A new yesterday, tomorrow

To this point, I studiously avoided reading any 'bestseller' titles of the sort that fill the discount bin at airport bookshops. (ever since I foolishly bought a copy of Chuffer Tomlinson's *A New Yesterday Tomorrow*) I only ever read books based on true stories, especially the autobiographies of the successful. The only exception was *Who moved my cheese?* by Spencer Johnson—a recommended read for all departments after our company announced the site move and outsourcing strategy.

Chapter 12

FOR SALE, 'GHOST OF A SMILE.' ONLY $499 WHILE STOCKS LAST!

In which: Peggy escapes the rat race, drinks champagne, opens a new life chapter, then sobs her heart out. Unemployment sinks in — Peggy realises she is 37 years of age and still doesn't know what she wants to do — Reflections on the necessity of having a plan B — The siren song of passive income — Ever onward! From failure to failure.

Beginning of the end

On my last day of employment, I left the office midday. I handed over my equipment and my badge and almost skipped to my car like a Maypole dancer. I sported a grin that would have given the Cheshire Cat a run for its money. Free at last, free at last, thank God almighty, we are free at last! (Yes, I know Martin Luther King Jr said it first, but that was precisely how I felt.)

Friday, and I'd arranged to go out that night with friends. We drank champagne to celebrate my escape from the rat race and to toast the start of a new chapter in my life. My newfound alcohol-fuelled happiness grew exponentially—right up until precisely 10 pm. Until then, I felt as if I was on a carnival float adorned with brightly coloured balloons. At 10:01 pm, however, my float burst a front tire, swerved up a side street and lurched sideways into a ditch. As stark reality turned my night of celebration into an emotional calamity, I broke down, sobbing.

I suddenly realised that I was unemployed. Worse, I had no plan for Monday. And if there was one day of the week that desperately needed a plan, it was Monday, especially this Monday.

I deliberately didn't look for another job because I could afford to take time off, and for the first time in years, I was able to walk my children to school. Previously, to get to work on time, I'd accelerate past the school gates at twice the speed limit before throwing wide the doors and 'helping' my beloved children out onto the pavement, with the sole of my Jimmy Choos.

Most of the time, they'd tumble through the school's entrance between the stone lions, having come to no harm. Mistimings occasionally resulted in one or t'other jamming their heads between the school railings, but wasn't that why the school had a nurse?

Employment 'suggestions'

Colleagues made redundant on the same day as me had new jobs to look forward to from Monday, or they already planned to work for themselves and consult. My plan was somewhat less enthusiastic. I would sign on at the Jobcentre once I dropped the kids at school. I suppose it had the advantage of simplicity. Emotionally, I felt as if a wrecking ball had knocked me over. I had not seen it coming. I felt lost.

I ruined the celebrations, of course. My husband had to call a taxi to get his mascara-smudged, hysterically-crying wife home. To this day, he has not forgiven me because it usually takes him a long time to get tipsy, whereas I needed a couple of glasses, and I'm gone, climbing the drapes to swing from the pelmet.

I might have anticipated my despair because this wasn't the first time I'd been devoid of a plan and feeling utterly hopeless. Back in the Stone Age, when I graduated, I had a mini-breakdown for the very same reasons.

I decided I was entitled to have a final summer off as a student and enjoy myself to infinity and beyond (to quote Buzz Lightyear). I planned to look for a job in September. Yet, many of my brighter classmates started employment in July, sacrificing their last ever summer holidays for a j.o.b. Seriously? Why would you? Fools. You will work for the rest of your lives. Duh?! No, thank you! Not interested. Include me out.

The thing about fun is that it's often best experienced with someone else. I had nobody to have fun with. They all had jobs. Including my best friend.

It was a lonely summer. Then September came, I signed on at the Jobcentre and broke down in despair.

Monday came around as it always does, and I walked to school with my two. Jobcentre was next on the agenda. I felt so ashamed to go. I didn't need the money, but I knew from one of the presentations I sat in during the redundancy process that having a gap in national insurance payments would impact my state pension, so they advised me to sign on at the Jobcentre regardless.

Luckily, the case manager assigned to me liked me. He gave me nine weeks to find a job of the same calibre and salary. After that, he would make 'Employment Suggestions' to me.

Employment Suggestions offer employment in jobs that you thought didn't exist outside of the ninth circle of hell. Strictly speaking, I could not be compelled to take one. It's just that not taking what they offered starved your state pension pot of contributions, practically guaranteeing an old age of fuel poverty, food banks, and eventually a pauper's funeral.

I had nine weeks to avoid this fate. This was one of the excellent benefits of working for a respectable employer; they allowed me to search for a decent job without pecking my head. To my annoyance, though, he said that to get my Job Seekers Allowance, which was circa seventy quid a week (and all of it mine to spend as I saw fit. Yaaaay!) I had to prove that I was actively searching, applying for jobs and attending interviews four hours a day.

Was this the trigger that turned me into an incapable, unambitious, non-entrepreneurial minion? It's hard to tell, but I started looking for any jobs that I sort of wouldn't mind doing. My get-up-and-go had got up and gone.

Geez! What was wrong with me? My CV was worthy of a nomination for the Nobel Prize for Resumes—so why was I thinking about becoming a postie?

Unnumbered, sure, but I genuinely considered any job without considering my value to the business community. Being unemployed made me feel worthless. All that personal development training, forgotten.

My mission was now to find a job before they found one for me. No way was I going to let anybody determine my future, but I was not exactly kind to myself.

What next?

I often wondered why I did not use all my free time (minus 4 hours of job hunting) to pursue my dream of being my own boss. All the personal development, all the prep before they released me into the big wide world; it all fell away the minute I stepped outside.

The problem was, it would have been easier to shuffle a deck of cards with one hand than decide what I wanted to do. I had a reasonably good idea of what I did not like and what I did not want to do (this category included wrestling with bears and crossing a minefield on a pogo stick) but identifying my niche was beyond my powers.

Thirty-seven years old, and I still did not know what I wanted to be! Pathetic! How do you expect high school kids to choose their GCSE subjects at the age of 12 when most adults do not know what they want to do with their lives? I considered jobs that did not involve sitting all day at a wood veneered, oak 'effect' desk. I was desperate to pick my hours and spend more time with the kids.

Apologies. I have strayed from network marketing. Instead, I seem to have shown you that I am not the go-getter I imagined.

Eventually, I found a decent job. This I considered in the same way as having my dental hygienist descale my teeth—a necessary evil without an ounce of pleasure. I quit with relish.

I then made a hefty withdrawal from my rapidly diminishing bank of courage reserves, set up a Limited company and started consulting. I had promoted myself from an employee to a contractor. It felt good to be my own boss to a certain degree. I no longer needed to do the typical corporate employee bullshit objectives and personal development plans I so hated (e.g. Objective 1: In six months, I will be third in the line of succession to the English throne.)

To be positive, although I was still in an office environment 9-5, I at least felt a little more fulfilled.

Plan B

The moral of this story is never to gamble with your career unless you have a plan B up your sleeve (tucked in your garter belt or even down your cleavage works too, but just have one—a plan B, I mean, not a cleavage.)

Enjoying a regular income meant that I could exploit a side hustle venture, and if it failed, I still had my job. The medium-term plan is to transform the side hustle into a full-time endeavour so that I could say good riddance to the day job. There were opportunities than a horse got hair, but knowing which one was a scam and which a benign business opportunity meant wading through a sea of YouTube videos for hours without end.

Stuff I did

- Googled 'How to make money online', 'Passive income opportunities'
- Read stacks of glowing testimonials, some so gushing I had to put on my Ray-Ban shades, in case their enthusiasm blinded me.
- Listened to webinars with fake interest
- I bought a super-inflated course (which promised eternal happiness and delivered the ghost of a smile.
- Joined a community of like-minded people all hungry for success.

Anybody who embarks on this journey will most likely follow the same strategy as I did, exploring the internet looking for anything avoiding an upfront cost or minimal capital. So, you look at drop shipping or buying stuff cheap in the shops and flipping it on Amazon or eBay for a profit.

If you could buy a Faberge egg for a quid at a car boot sale and sell it on Alibaba for two million yen, good luck to you, but I suspect margins were generally tighter.

I bought a domain for the same price as a No 7 lipstick and found somebody on Fiverr to build me an Amazon Affiliate site. I convinced myself that l would need to order rubble sacks to store my profits. That everybody from commoners to royalty would flock to my page, click on the products, get directed to my Amazon site, and Amazon would reward me big-stylee for drawing users to them like the Pied Piper of Hamelin. (Cue Dire Straits, *Money for Nothing* and tango around the room like they'd cancelled tomorrow!)

Five years on, and I am still waiting for my first commission payment. No lie!

Sigh

Like with any business, they made it all sound as easy as peeling a banana. The people who should have told me that it wasn't enough just to have a live site—it needed to be optimised too, never told me. They never said to me that the user had to be able to find it. If anyone knows the whereabouts of these people, please get in touch—I'm offering a reward.

Every man and his German Shepherd can buy a domain these days and build a website. The key is to be search engine optimised so that people can find your website in the first place. D'oh. But you live and learn. Or fail and learn.

As Albert Einstein said, 'Anyone who has never made a mistake has never tried anything new.' The rumour is that he said this after losing his shirt to some physicist pals in his first-ever game of Gin Rummy. Winston Churchill also had something to say on the subject: 'Success consists of going from failure to failure without loss of enthusiasm.' I have this one in bold and capitals pasted to my fridge as a reminder.

Chapter 13

ADVICE BY THE CUBIC MILE

In which: Peggy finds the actual cost of side ventures — Builds a personal MLM book collection to rival the US Library of Congress — Discovers the wonders of Audible, the greatest invention since the Walnut Whip! — Realises that Jill-of-all-trades is an obsolete strategy to millionaire dreams.

You can't beat a good book

Every new side-hustle venture came with a metric ton of advice, a dumper truck of new material and learning, a slew of private FB groups and networks of people. I was not typically the most active participant in those groups, but I definitively bookmarked, saved and took on what others were recommending.

I was an onlooker, a spectator taking silent actions behind the scenes, like a virtuous version of an agent provocateur. These groups inspired me to buy enough personal development books to open a high street book shop.

Some of these volumes were good, some had a profound effect on me, and some were so far above my mental capacity that I felt like a chimpanzee trying to read the Old Testament. I liked most of them. The ones that failed to shake me were those whose advice I could not implement.

Take a famous title like *The 4-Hour Workweek* by Tim Ferriss. Many budding entrepreneurs raved about Tim's Magnum opus. I couldn't see how to apply the real wisdom between the covers of this book unless the reader already worked for themselves, which was already a better position to the 9-5 wage slaves who worked for a boss in a sedentary job.

Interesting reads stuffed my bookshelves. I collected books like trophies, but I hardly ever implemented any advice because I got bogged down in the next book, like a dinosaur in a tar pit. At least one speaker at every event hammered home the message that 'Action was the foundational key to all success.' You must take massive action. Stop wishing, start doing. It would help if you gained momentum.

If you want my book recommendation, read *The Snowball: Warren Buffett and the business of life* by Alice Schroeder or *The Compound Effect* by Darren Hardy. The Snowball was way above my capacity to grasp its labyrinthine complexities. But I understood the principle of what the author was trying to say. The Compound Effect was in plain English, clear, and concise. Both books talk about momentum—an essential concept in the MLM world.

I like Darren, so I subscribed to DarrenDaily, which is like daily mentoring sessions delivered directly to your mailbox.

I used to listen to him whilst I was preparing the kids' packed lunches. The tiny injection of positivity first thing in the morning felt fabulous. An excellent start to the day. Besides, he's a handsome little devil (There, I've said it!)

The problem was, I had more books on my 'must read or die' list than I could possibly read before I ran smack bang into another highly recommended book. The situation was dire: I had a backlog of books, never implementing a single thing, and constantly felt I still had so much to learn.

Viva la (Audible) revolution!

And then Audible came into my life! (Cue SFX of the Hallelujah Chorus!) Free at last, free at last, good God almighty, I'm free at last! I could now listen to books whilst getting dragged around the park by the dog, commuting to work, doing chores. It was revolutionary. Viva la revolution!

In one of Rob Moore's books, he talks about listening to hundreds of audiobooks a year, and he listens to them at double speed to get through more books quickly. Pro tip! I experimented with 1,5 x speed at first, got used to it and then moved to 2 x speed. Absolutely ground-breaking advice until I decided to purchase Kevin Hart's *I can't make this up. Life lessons.* Pff! That man speaks 2 x speed in everyday life! I couldn't tell you what his life lessons were!

Also, the law of diminishing returns applies here. Why not listen at triple speed? Or even faster. I listened to 'War and Peace' once, at 50 times the average rate? I heard the whole book in one minute, 15.4 seconds. It sounded like two dolphins discussing Korean reunification.

Now I have a collection of audiobooks. I got through loads more material, but I still wasn't taking any action. Maybe I have not come across a book that moved me, or maybe there was something wrong with me? Any audiobook that I loved and wanted to take action on, I purchased in paperback too, so that I could revisit it to highlight important points, scribble marginal notes like a pro and remind myself of the beneficial stuff.

Guess how many times I did this! Go on, guess. What's that you say? Z-e-r-o. I did exactly what I said up to the point of revising and using the book as a textbook. So now I had a paperback on the bookshelf as well as a copy in my audio library.

Hold the front page!

I made a breakthrough. I listened to them several times, and that brought an improvement! I finally found a few books that grabbed my attention. Nope, they were not manuals on recruiting into your organisation or how to meditate, eat well, sleep well and get up at dark o'clock to grind through another day. No preaching. Books filled the gaps in my understanding of specific topics I did not manage to figure out for myself. Some of those were just eye-opening 'reads' or the 'kick in the butt' I needed.

Outliers by Malcolm Gladwell was a fascinating listen. Malcolm Gladwell analysed the reasons that contributed to high levels of success. He talked about The Beatles, Bill Gates and other intriguing topics. Still, ultimately his study concluded that the key to achieving outstanding proficiency in any skill was, to a great extent, a matter of practising the right way, for a total of around 10,000 hours. (Okay, that means I'm not going to be a millionaire any time soon)

Success was not about 'being in the right place at the right time', or 'what's for you will never go by you'. Nor any other strand of home-spun mumbo-jumbo straight from the pages of your great grandma's almanack of explanations for life based on a heady blend of superstition and pure ignorance. Anyone coming out on top had put in the hours.

Practice, practice, practice! I drum this into my kids when they want to give up. I told my eldest only last week:

ME: The key to success is practice. Now go back into the garden and shoot some more hoops.

ELDEST: But mum, it's midnight, and it's pitch black out there.

ME: That's why Santa brought you that luminous basketball for Christmas.

Deliberate practice. Lightbulb moment numero uno!

'Think and Grow Rich' (and other helpful titles)

Think and Grow Rich by Napoleon Hill was always popular with hardcore entrepreneurs. The kind of people who could sell doormats to the homeless and walk away smiling. The title went down well whether you wanted to sell stuff on Amazon, run a network marketing business, or corner the export market to Bolivia in wholesale pork scratchings. If you were interested in making your fortune, this book must have pride of place on your bookshelf.

Think and Grow Rich was a personal development and self-improvement book, written in 1937 but remarkably still relevant, and I uncovered lots of valuable nuggets in its pages. I have listened to this book four times now. It fascinates me to know that this kind of material was already available in the 40s!

How Not to Die by Dr Michael Greger was an accidental purchase. I don't mean I walked into Waitrose intent on buying Pop-Tarts, but somehow left with this audiobook, but I often bought the most expensive books I could find on Audible with my monthly credit. And since I was in a health and wellness MLM, almost brainwashed into thinking my food only ever came in the powdered form, it was refreshing to listen to Dr Michael Greger talk about his nutrition research.

His scientific research proves that what you eat can prevent and reverse many of the causes of disease-related deaths. It seemed that simple changes to diet and lifestyle could save you from premature death (If ever offered the choice of death, don't tick the box that says, 'premature'. Almost any other kind is to be preferred. Just saying.)

Dr Greger only eats plant-based food, and he also has a checklist (daily dozen) that tells you what you should include in your daily diet, which I find incredibly useful.

Roasted Kabocha with Kale-Cranberry Stuffing, anyone?

One of Dr Greger's recipes is for the exotically named 'Roasted Kabocha with Kale-Cranberry Stuffing.' Those willing to fly to Tokyo in pursuit of a kabocha (it's a Japanese variety of pumpkin) and able to get back in time for their guests arriving say it tastes a bit like lovely chestnuts. If you're thinking of trying this out, bear in mind that a single kabocha can weigh eight pounds, so when pricing your meal, be sure to include 10 Yen for the Kabocha and £140 for excess baggage.

It's tempting to assume that anyone said by anyone living on alfalfa sprouts, coconut water and corn husks should be disregarded as the ravings of a maniac. Yet, there was no disputing that he backed up everything he said with a complete scientific pedigree. What's more, his website is a non-commercial, science-based public service providing free updates on the latest news in nutrition research via bite-sized videos. A persuasive platform indeed.

I have even downloaded his Daily Dozen app to keep me in check, although I already know by heart what healthy choices I should be making now, including the ideal legume-to-berry ratio for my height. And I know enough about cruciferous vegetables to be considered a world authority on the subject. I even applied to the BBC Mastermind programme, stating my specialist subject: 'The role of cruciferous vegetables in the Suffragette Movement 1903-1904.' I was beaten in the finals by a fellow from Stockport who specialised in Dot Cotton from Eastenders. C'est la vie.

If you fancy a different kind of audiobook to personal development or icebreakers for MLM prospects, check it out. And don't forget the Pro-tip! 2 x speed.

The perils of self-narration

You sure will need to crank up the speed if you hope to subject yourself to Dr Michael Greger, who narrates his own titles. Because, unfortunately, Dr Greger's narrative style doesn't precisely bounce along like a sailor's hornpipe. You could mimic his narrative voice by first staying awake for three days, then swallowing 100 mg of diazepam (those with interest in pharmacology, please note that 50 mg is enough to stop a charging hippo in its tracks). To finish off the impersonation using the correct emotional tone, read out the name of every man who perished building the Burma Railroad between 1943 and 1945.

I was hesitant to buy *Just F*cking Do It* by Noor Hibbert because I have somehow been disappointed by female entrepreneur books before. Especially those that have obscene titles or are trying to toughen you up for the big world as if you were subordinate. It was finally your time to shine. I am sure there are plenty of good ones out there, but I've not been fortunate enough to come across one yet.

But it must have been recommended yet again, so I checked it out on Amazon, read the reviews and bought it. Boy, am I glad I did! It was not the actual Just F*cking Do It that made me get off my butt; it was the fact that the author's life and the whole process of becoming a happy, successful version of herself resembled my trail of thinking and the journey I was on. I could identify with this woman.

I felt that she and I had so much in common. It gave me hope to learn that many others felt the same way. It also made me realise that she was a doer and part of a unique band of individuals with perseverance deep in their DNA.

Long after ordinary mortals like you and me had worked ourselves into a hissy fit because we couldn't find the end of the Sellotape after 30 seconds of random scratching with our last unbroken nail, she'd still be demonstrating the art of not giving up.

She tried everything for 'real'. She went all in. If she did not like it, she moved on to the next thing. I tried everything in 'my head' or 'toe-dipped', didn't like it, moved on to the next thing. I was not doing; I was an amateur, a dabbler.

Yikes

During this process, she discovered her niche, and she is now a successful qualified life and business coach. This book has practical steps to improve your life, make positive changes in your life and live the life you deserve.

And finally, the book that gave the most uncomplicated advice on the most complex subject. Lightbulb moment numero dos! *The ONE Thing* by Gary Keller and Jay Papasan. Who remembers writing their CVs straight out from school, with zero job experience? What did you write as your strengths? 'Flexible, organised multitasker?'

The world has always required us to multitask as employees, colleagues, mothers, and wives. We are so proud that we can multitask. We cook and wash at the same time. We take on several projects in tandem. We are on conference calls whilst replying to emails, self-administering a pedicure and buttering crumpets. We can do more than one thing at a time. But guess what, it's not good.

This book wasn't the first to extol the virtues of focusing on one thing at a time. I even preached to my kids that they should focus on the task at hand without any distractions, though this produced mixed results:

ME: Children, your mummy has been practising narrowing her mind beam to focus single-mindedly and with laser-like precision on the task in hand. And she would like you to do the same (Short pause) with your homework!

KID 1: Yes, mummy? (Whispering to her sibling): Oh God, she's talking about herself in the third person again. Should we call dad?

KID 2: What a smashing idea, mummy! (Whispering back to her sibling): The last time, she made us practice mindfulness while tidying up our bedrooms.

Sometime later, during the same day...

ME: Well, children, how's the focus going?

KID 1: Great, mummy. We decided to put all of our efforts into finding and eating every last piece of chocolate in the house. We finished off the chocolate coins from last Christmas, gobbled down handfuls of Galaxy Counters, and we even found the two-litre tub of Ferrero Rocher you thought nobody knew you had stashed under the stairs. We nearly missed the catering pack of Toffifee under the floorboards. The kilogram of cooking chocolate wasn't great, but we had half each and managed to keep it down. Didn't we do well, mummy?

ME: And the homework?

KID 1: Homework?

ME: And where's your little sister?

KID 1: Ah, she's in the upstairs loo, throwing up. Quite spectacularly, actually.

Yet, I could not master this simple concept myself! I feared that if I did not do more than one thing at the time, I would turn into a Spam fritter—well, okay, there was no magical thinking involved, but I did feel as if time would fly by too quickly.

So I tried to cram as much into the spare time I had and ended up failing at everything simply because I couldn't focus properly on just one single thing. There were too many shiny objects on display along my entrepreneurial journey. The more FB groups I belonged to, the more I learnt about the next craze or technology—the wind-powered draft excluder or whatever.

I felt 'I must do it now because if I'm in at the inception of this, the latest hypnotically shiny object, surely I, and I alone have the greatest chance of taking the lead'.

Sigh

The perils of toe-dipping

How stupid of me. This book was just what I needed. I look back, and years have passed since my redundancy, and in the intervening gap, I'd toe-dipped into too many things without mastering one.

The most upsetting part was, I knew if I grasped something, if I got good at something, I would be brilliant. This was already a proven facet of my work ethic. I had been thrown in the deep end many times before. Although sometimes I had a rocky start, I always came out of the situation as an expert!

Why wasn't I capable of doing this for myself? Go on, Einstein, I said to myself, answer that if you dare! So frustrating. Nobody's perfect, of course. At least I had arrived at this understanding now and not on my deathbed! Was there a reason why I always seemed to take the difficult path? As my Reiki master (a story for another day) always told me, there is a divine timing for all things.

And by the way, to all the young students or entrepreneurs who understand the mastery of the One thing, kudos, you have my utmost admiration. I am making sure my kids focus on The ONE Thing!

I read and listened to many more books that were invaluable, and I have adopted the wisdom of one or two. But the more books I bought, the more I realised that they all said the same thing. They were all pretty much adaptations of Think and Grow Rich or *The Secret*, a book by Rhonda Byrne worth mentioning, although it may not be everybody's cup of tea. I have had this book for 15 years, and it's still only partially read (So I'm a slow reader. So what?)

A friend recommended it to me, but I was not ready for it, so it just gathered dust on my bookshelf. The Secret is a compilation of interviews with leading authors, philosophers, scientists, and others, in which it discussed the Law of Attraction. The message of The Secret is that you can create your reality (Yes, I know that sounds a bit X-Files, but stick with me, you might learn something, I watched the whole movie on YouTube.)

The idea is that we are each in charge of our destiny; our thoughts can become things. You are what you manifest. It is the best-selling self-help guide out there, and I suggest you start with this classic and Think and Grow Rich because everybody's self-help and personal development books are adapted versions of these two sourcebooks.

Hopefully, I have saved you some cash, but I understand sometimes you appreciate things only from a certain point of view and from a specific author who can explain them in a way you understand. It's like looking back over your school years. My maths teacher was a genius in his subject. He memorised logarithm tables for fun and worked out a mental method for calculating the square root of his social security number. But he could not speak my language. A friend of mine could explain it to me in words I understood, and voila! All of a sudden, it made perfect sense.

Recycled material

If to motivate yourself, you continuously read insightful books; you deny yourself those a-ha! moments at the next MLM event. You realise that the training is heavily based on those self-help and personal development books. I naïvely considered the company's coaches geniuses. Wise beyond words! Capable of levitation, or getting their doctor to make a house call on a weekend, and other semi-impossible things.

In my first event, I was in my element; I was writing everything down faster than a speeding bullet, taking pictures of PowerPoint presentations and recording all the clever nuggets of entrepreneurial wisdom they were sharing. I was sold! At least on the personal development part.

It took me the best part of a year to realise that I was just a newbie, and in the next event, another millionaire mentor would share a presentation with the same nuggets served on a different platter. And of course, I was already absorbing personal development and self-help books through literature and listening to audios, so it was hard to hear something new.

But then you were guilt-tripped for failing to identify a new 'take-away' from the current presentation. Especially as the trainer would often call out another millionaire mentor from the audience. The chosen one would proclaim that her information was the most valuable piece of advice they had heard in a lifetime of wheeling-dealing. At least since their granny told them never to ask the dealer for another card in Blackjack when sitting on twenty.

I found this a bit, Am-Dram, recycled. Still, maybe to be a successful MLM associate, you had to ham it up now and again. I guess they did this for the benefit of the newbies, who had come to their first event. And because although I was no longer a newbie, neither was I a seasoned pro. I was an in-betweener. I felt confused, silly, and hopeless, believing the most likely explanation was that I had not paid enough attention during the presentation.

Chapter 14

EVERY DAY'S A SCHOOL DAY – SO RING THAT BELL

In Which: Peggy unearths the tribal nature of MLM leadership — Learns the gazillion Do's and Don'ts (Well, some of them anyway) — learns to hate the protocol of posting to private pages — Blows her psychic overload fuse — Through a rush of ambition to the head, amasses 100 terabytes of sales information — Her personal Facebook page sinks like an anvil in a bathtub, and dies memberless.

Do you want to be in our tribe?

Following some close observations, I noticed that all great leaders had their own following, their own faithful tribes. Not the sort of tribes once popular in BBC documentaries back in the sixties, featuring a bloke with a Guinea fowl leg-bone through his nose and a circular bread-board in his lip, and braless women hunched over metal cooking pots—not that sort of tribe. The other sort.

The sort I ended up in. My upline had invited me to join a Facebook group run by a mentor whose tribe, apparently, I now belonged to. With immediate effect, their rules applied to me, like it or not. Had I belonged to a tribe of Stone Age hunter-gatherers, I might have been put in charge of gathering berries or digging up edible roots. This successful, thoroughly modern tribe had around 50,000 participants. And no one was required to pick a single berry nor poke around in the topsoil for truffles—we just sent out for a Greggs Steak Slice at lunchtimes.

This tribe had business builders, product users and nosey, curtain-twitching types we called 'prospects'. Basically, inviting them to the group was a step closer to getting them signed up. The person who founded this private Facebook page was many layers up in my upline. She reached millionaire status during my MLM journey, so I knew what she preached worked.

I was grateful I belonged to some team because all newbies needed to 'watch and learn'—to start from ground zero as it were. Curiously, I experienced no sense of belonging because everything was pretty overwhelming. Still, my fellow business builders were friendly and kind and made me feel more of a welcome participant than a neglected trainee.

The gazillion do's and dont's

The complicated part came with learning the tribe's mandatory rituals and prohibitions—their DO's and DON'Ts. There were gazillions of them! Had you laid them tail to toe in a single line, they would have reached too far, far away and back again (sorry, I can't be more precise.)

So not only was I trying to learn the compensation plan, understand the process, learn about the products and everything else, and learn the etiquette around posting to this private page. Just as once you'd have been birched and sent to bed early for eating peas off your fish knife, so too did we need to mind our online Ps and Qs—the etiquette for sending and responding to tribal communications.

There was a separate, similarly-titled Private FB page exclusively for business builders, where these rules were reinforced with a rod of iron and a fist of steel, or possibly the other way round (Geez, I'm beginning to scare myself now!) My FB pages catalogue was growing!

Haddock-Smoking kilns

There was just too much information for one human to compute. I felt like one of those pioneering astronauts in the early days of space travel, having their resilience tested by shaking them out of a deep sleep at three in the morning, strapping them into a centrifuge, subjecting them to six gees, before hanging them upside down by their bare feet in a haddock-smoking kiln, and forcing them to do endless Sudoku puzzles with a blunt pencil.

Simone thought that she'd make it easy for me by sharing, via Dropbox, her entire collection of information from these FB pages and elsewhere, tracing back to the beginning of time. Sweet mother of God, there were folders, subfolders, sub-sub folders, documents, pictures, spreadsheets, templates. Welsh coal mines dating back to the 18th century had fewer levels.

This was ludicrous! I could not possibly read all this. It was like somebody's handover notes that had been dropped into a wind tunnel then haphazardly re-assembled. We all use different methods to file our information, and it's always easier to do it with your own documents, or at least something you either read, created or wrote yourself. Time for me to 'fess up. Sorry Simone, but I never read the stuff. I appreciated the kind gesture to help me on my journey, and I'm sure it made sense to you, but I started my own collection!

So very ambitiously, I began studying material from the company's official websites, training tools, all the tutorials on the private pages. I saved all the essential info to my folder and my phone. So it was at my fingertips if I was out and about and couldn't get to my computer. It was information overload; I was obsessed with collecting new information. My folders started to resemble Simone's.

Ouch

OneNote and Hashtag Central

But, as the book of Ecclesiastes (7:15) says: *Fear ye not!* So I didn't.

I came out with a new strategy. I have been happily, and may I say, successfully using OneNote during my day job. So I decided that since I am serious about this MLM malarky, I would treat it as such, so I created OneNote with all the fancy tabs and subtabs and organised my info in the order of a life cycle of an MLM prospect that anyone could follow.

I covered every step of the journey from initial contact to what to say, what to text, how to respond, inviting them to the private page, welcoming them to the group, getting them on the three-way call, and closing a sale.

I had fancy tabs for all the career stages from associate to the highest rank, what you needed to know and what one's objection was to progress to the next step. I had another tab, including a phone album titled 'social', full of motivational quotes, which I used to create my fancy FB and IG posts. I would go on free image websites to find royalty-free images of the highest quality, added a custom font that I used on all my pictures, used the quote from the saved album, saved it and created posts on social media.

My project became hashtag central; I added tons of them, for which I had a separate 'folder' titled fitness, health, wealth, family, or other topics that

I had already researched, copied, and pasted. Job done. I had a system. I was as proud as a mummy squirrel whose babies (squirrel-ettes?) had just climbed to the top of a pine tree for the first time on their own. I started to create my brand, and my picture quotes were recognisable because they were consistent, and they all looked professional.

As I got good at it, some of the MLM guys in my friend's list started to repost my material. Grrr! I should have been delighted that people found my stuff good enough to repost, but I felt upset because I did all the spade-work. But then I gave myself a stern talking to. Reminding myself that I also reposted stuff, and this was no different, so I wound my neck back in and took comfort in the fact that I'd done a good enough job for others to share.

My own private Facebook page

I decided to emulate the successful leaders by creating my own private FB Page. I called it 'Rise to Success' and started to save a truckload of helpful information for my 'apprentices' to use. Yet clearly, my thinking remained bogged down in a false belief that I still knew far too little. So I continued to learn, adding more and more info.

Sadly, my page never took off. To be fair, I don't think I was cut out for the role of 'Administrator General' of a group, policing what goes on, ensuring everyone was happy and toeing the line. It also irritated me that these FB groups were more straightforward to create than a corned beef sandwich. Every man and his dog (his name's Pivo, I think) now had a FB group. All they needed to do was just hit 'invite all friends', and you ended up with hundreds of pending invitations to join private groups.

I supported my friends—the real people I knew and that, through joining their group, I had met in person, with their little business ventures, but another MLM private group was too much for me. So, although I continued to build my private group, I could not bring myself to let people know about it because I hated it so much myself.

This reminded me of the workman who, each day, sat down to lunch in the factory dining hall and then face-palmed himself each time he opened his lunch box. 'OMG! Not cheese again!' He complained.

'Why don't you ask the wife to make you salami sandwiches for a change?' a workmate asked the man on Friday.

'That's not going to help much,' the man grumbled, 'I make them myself.'

Some FB groups required no permission to join. You were involuntarily added. Brutal. This was the trick to gaining more members. This might explain how the leading group grew rapidly to 66K + in headcount before I left, two years after joining. Although the rules were evident in the group's defence, we had to ask permission from the prospect first if they wanted to be invited. It was a no-no to add anybody we could think of.

However, these hungry copycats, who took 'duplication' and 'don't reinvent the wheel' to higher levels, added just about anybody they knew, including their MLM chums, to their private FB groups, whether they wanted to be added had nothing to do with it. Their primary objective was to grow rapidly, expand and show a higher count of members.

They also wanted your moral support, or shall I say, requested it outright. They instructed us to comment and like their posts to help them achieve a wider reach. What made me laugh—erm, cringe, was the plagiarism. Oh, dear! Sharing is caring? Yeah, right! There was a reason why some people were successful! They were original! By all means, imitate, don't copy and paste. It's wrong, bad and obvious.

But then Facebook rode to the rescue on a white charger like Sir Lancelot (three cheers for FB!), bestowing enhanced rules on all burgers of the kingdom of MLM (OK, that's enough of that nonsense!) governing who can be invited to a group and if they were an active participant. If you have been added to a group without your knowledge or consent, and if you've never visited that group, you would be removed automatically. All invitations had to be accepted by the person who was being invited.

This caused a kind of panic and anxiety amongst business builders, not seen since stockholders started a craze for cordless bungee-jumping, from the highest window ledges on Wall Street in 1930. These business builders feared that this might limit the numbers of participants they would be able to add successfully to the group. Some invited prospects left, right and centre because even if they consented to be added, without their approval, they never made it into the group and therefore could not be indoctrinated.

I used to be indecisive, but now I'm not so sure

In addition to my shiny notes, fancy posters, laminated price lists, I printed all the information in a logical order and put it all in a binder with colourful dividers. Another stupid idea of mine, because I ended up with an angry husband who had to order more print cartridges from Amazon! (Psst! Can you keep a secret? Don't tell him, but I never used that binder.)

Whatever possessed me to do this, I will never know. Had I inadvertently annoyed a voodoo priestess? Whatever the reason, it was not my brightest moment. Maybe it was a prime example of procrastination? I said it before, and I'll repeat it, procrastination is a bitch.

I don't want to get technical with you here, but procrastination avoids a task that needs to be accomplished by a specific deadline (OK, so I Googled it! So what?) It can also be a habitual or intentional delay to starting or finishing a task despite knowing it might have negative consequences (Wikipedia).

What was I avoiding, though? Was I deliberately keeping myself 'busy' as an excuse not to meet and network with new prospects (displacement behaviour) while at the same time reporting to my upline that I was busier than a counter assistant at a Primark January sale?

To continue with my psychoanalysis (it's pretty good fun, actually), I avoided this because I could not surmount my objections with MLM? And therefore, by not talking to more people, I didn't have to pretend that this was the best opportunity since Margaret Thatcher floated British Gas. Because I believed it as much as I thought that fairies at the bottom of our garden looked after our gooseberry bush while we slept?

As you probably already guessed, my FB page, though stuffed full of helpful info, remained resolutely memberless. However, I had lots of shiny handover notes ready for my keen business builders—if only I could recruit any.

So far, I had only been able to attract customers to my downline. They were all happy product users seeing positive results, so I just needed to convince some of them to start sharing their results with their friends and tempt them into joining our excellent company. If only my customers could get two customers of their own, they would get promoted with a bonus, and more to the point, I would get promoted with a bonus. Everybody wins, and the lives of a few more people would be changed for the better. Yippee!

Naïve question: 'Was that difficult?'

Brutally realistic answer: 'Fuck, yeah!'

They constantly reminded us of the company's mantras, 'You can't say a wrong thing to the right person.' This I would believe when the right person stood before me more often than the wrong person.

You could say that Lady Luck had her arm around my shoulder because those that bragged about their results and attracted friends to try our products were only too happy to refer them to me. They preferred this to recruit them themselves, even with my support, into their downline. They could have had a bonus and paid for their next order, but they did not want the hassle and asked me to take care of them. Result!

Chapter 15

'SAINT' KATHERINE, PATRON SAINT OF LOST MLM PRACTITIONERS

In which: Network-thriving Katherine, the perfect partner, comes to Peggy's life — The best-laid plans of mice and men fall off the edge of the planet and get eaten by dragons as Katherine shows an allergic reaction to the product! — Data of allergic reactions turns out to be rarer than rocking horse poop — Peggy and her perfect partner drift apart.

Katherine

Lady Luck put her other arm around my shoulder (it's a wonder I could still breathe!) when I found somebody interested in building the business with me. Maybe I manifested her into my life, but I certainly spent long hours hunting down the missing puzzle pieces in my quest for success. I had become a latter-day Mrs Marbles from an Agatha Crispy novel (Note to editor: please check this reference)

I did all the right things, but I still did not have the guts to put myself out there. I felt lonely in my business. Something Simone once told me a while back: Many successful millionaires were couples that both bought into this business model. Either that or one started, and the other joined them when they caught the same vision or reluctantly dragged them into it involuntarily.

That seemed to be the impression I got from Simone and Karl. Simone was the driver; Karl, the reluctant spouse. Unfortunately, I had more of a chance of getting a member of the Amish community to buy a fidget spinner off me than convincing my other half to become a business builder. He was in it solely for the shakes, and that was that. He had zero interest in building the business, plus he thought someone was brainwashing me. Credit where it is due, though, he supported me throughout my journey. He believed in me. He never tried to talk me out of it, and I probably wouldn't have let him because I thought it was possible.

So how did I meet Katherine, my one and only business builder? Don't laugh. Actually, laugh all you want! It almost sounds made up. It was through another Psychic, our Reiki master Mandy! She lived locally, and me and the kids visited her monthly. She is like a mother to me, and I enjoy our regular visits. We click. She shows genuine interest in the kids and me, and we always overrun the hourly sessions. She has learnt not to book any subsequent sessions because she enjoys our company as much as we enjoy hers.

Don't worry, my spare room isn't full of specialist psychics, at my beck and call, day and night. I don't have one that reads chicken entrails, another that reads tea leaves (or do they read tea bags nowadays?), and a third who's a wiz on the tarot cards.

This time I wanted to ask, 'Will my efforts be rewarded?' I booked myself in for a reading, minus the kids. We chatted before we settled down to business, she politely asked me about my shakes, and I told her what I had realised over the last few weeks of intense thinking and mind-beam focusing: I needed a partner, like toast required butter.

I realised that I could not do this alone. I needed somebody to compliment my strengths—someone whose strengths balanced my weaknesses. I needed somebody confident, outgoing and didn't mind talking to strangers—Hello Katherine!

The name came to Mandy as if by magic. Mandy is a medium (I don't mean in terms of dress size, I mean in her ability to reach out 'beyond the veil'); Katherine could have been anybody who wanted to connect with me. From what I gather, the spirit world (Enter through death's door, fly across the wild blue yonder, to the Great Beyond, then exit at the next junction) is more crowded than the 80% off section at a Primark sale. Mandy reckoned a lot of the departed got bored quickly with eternity and lined up to help people like me in the mortal realm.

But I knew of nobody called Katherine. The more we talked, the more it became clear to Mandy that she knew Katherine and that she was the partner I was looking for. In Mandy's exact words, 'Katherine could sell sand to the Arabs'.

I liked the sound of that! Was this the perfect partner I was hoping for? I could do all the preparation, arranging, organising, and she could be the spokesperson. Mandy's insights were never the result of slaughtering a chicken and poking its gizzard about with a soup spurtle. Still, she was superb at conjuring the right name out of clean air when the occasion demanded without uttering a single abracadabra or hocus pocus.

Katherine would know how to break the ice, and once broken, I could join in the conversation. You probably think I'm a chicken. I suppose I am! But seriously, I get suspicious when people act coy and stare at their shoes to avoid eye contact. Then twenty minutes later, they're cavorting about a stage in front of hundreds of people like a seasoned Can-Can dancer, shamelessly flashing the gusset of her Oo-Lah-Lah bloomers to hundreds of unseated strangers in the upper circle.

I knew that if I got going with Katherine, it would take some practice, but I would eventually warm up. Besides, she was an experienced salesperson running a successful business with her husband. But she complained to Mandy that she couldn't be more bored if she tried to memorise a knitting pattern for a Fair Isle Jumper. She even knew what network marketing was; bonus! And she previously worked for a nutritional company! Hallelujah!

There'd be no need for sweet-talking, especially since I was so bad at it. Before she'd even unboxed the tarot cards, Mandy called Katherine on her mobile to tell her what just happened and why she was calling her. The next thing I knew, I was talking directly to her, explaining what I did and that I was looking to partner up with somebody like her.

The conversation flowed easily because Mandy introduced me and set the scene. Although I did wonder what must have gone through Katherine's mind after the phone call, she, like me, was an opportunist, and we arranged to meet in my house the following night.

I was blown away by how easily it went. I could not have been more flabbergasted had the Tooth Fairy knocked on my door and said, 'I still owe you eight quid for your milk teeth. Here's a tenner, keep the change.'

I would have never met Katherine if I had not gone to see Mandy that night, so I began to think I had conjured her into my life. The tarot cards also gave me a very positive financial forecast (with a margin of error of +/- 5%). I truly believed that finally, my boat had come in. I would eventually make it with my new partner!

During Katherine's visit, we got to know each other a bit better. I gave her a summary of my MLM journey and why I would like to partner up with her. She said she thrived on talking to people, and it did not bother her to network at all. Music to my ears. And since she was happy to join me and be my partner, we set up her business account and ordered her products. She told me about her previous company and their products, and I felt like a seven-year-old on Christmas Eve.

We kept in touch daily, and I drip-fed information to her via the FB groups and postings. We met up for coffee regularly and talked. I was so grateful for her arrival in my life because I had gained a friend who was on the same wavelength as me. The more we talked, the more I realised how much we had in common, except for the fact that she was successful, and I was not—a discrepancy I was keen to remedy.

As usual, I was harder on myself than one of those medieval penitents who wore the horsehair shirts. I may have been a failure in many of the 'side hustle' adventures I embarked on, but I was pretty successful in my corporate career and life in general. And for that, I was grateful because it enabled me to play and experiment on the side. But we are never happy with what we have and want more, would you agree?

I found Katherine fascinating, and I loved our face to face meetings. She used to tell me about her life, how she travelled as far as the US for self-development and personal development seminars, she was hungry to learn, coachable—cue heavenly choir—and she was a risk-taker. She even did the Fire Walk at one of Tony Robbins events. I was impressed. I had landed up with a partner, but I also got somebody to look up to. Finally!

Why can you never find the antihistamine when you need it?

However, the Lord (or whoever pulls the levers up there) moves, they say, in mysterious ways. Because one of the wheels on my personal divine plan—the one with my name in gold embossed calligraphy— fell off. My partner turned out to be the first-ever customer to experience an adverse reaction to the products. She broke out in horrendous menopause-quality hot flushes as soon as she started taking the products—suddenly feeling as if she'd been sitting in a steam cabinet for a long weekend. This was precisely the sort of thing that convinced me that nobody unqualified should call themselves a Nutritional Coach or any other similarly ridiculous title.

We were not experts. I could barely talk with authority on the possible side effects of soluble aspirin. We promoted nutritional products. We were the product users. At least the majority of us, because if you Googled 'Salad Dodgers' Hall of Fame' and clicked on 'images', you'd see a group panorama photo of at least half a dozen weight-challenged MLM nutritional millionaires. They all looked like they were best buddies with Ronald McDonald.

If they used the products, they would all be lean, healthy, and have more energy than a crate of Duracell batteries. But they obviously could talk the hind legs off an elk without the need to 'be the product of the product' to make the sale.

I tried frantically to give Katherine answers. I was doing it all wrong, but there is no way I would follow protocol. You were supposed to find the relevant FB post in the group with a person with the same issue. Then tag the person in it so that they can read it for themselves. You were supposed to find a relevant article on the company website and send the link to them.

This was faintly absurd. Imagine a similarly minded doctor arriving on the scene of a horrific RTA. There's a bloke with his head hanging over to one side like a zombie. 'Help me, doc,' he croaks.

'Don't worry,' the doctor says, 'I'm faxing you a fact sheet with my top five hacks and tips on major head trauma.'

I wanted to find a solution for her, so I frantically read everything I could on this subject and then messaged her suggestions.

The problem was that articles about adverse reactions to products were more challenging to find than rocking horse poop. Why? Negative feedback doesn't get sales. What you see on the website is sufficient to a degree because they described each product in detail and any known reactions or sensations you might experience (ears falling off when exposed to sunlight, growing an extra toe, and so on—just joking!)

But like any other products sold in the UK, they had to comply with strict label requirements. Ingredients had to be listed on the product label, and anything that was a known allergen, printed in bold. The thing was that I did not understand all the fancy ingredients, so I could not figure out which of the many products she took each day was causing the hot flushes. And pleeeease! There is no way that in an FB group of 66,000+ participants, nobody had encountered this? She could not have been the first one.

The ingredients for success

The scientific language used on the product labels got to me this time. I began having a recurring dream. In the dream, I read the information leaflet that came with one of the products. It was the size of an army blanket and dense with peculiar ingredients. The more I read, the crazier the list got.

The product descriptions started on the familiar ground because the first ingredient was 'aqua', water. No problem there, unless Katherine was allergic to H2O! But from the very next ingredient, the list headed for the dark side and never once looked back.

Lawnmower grease, Shake n Vac, turpentine, Cillit Bang, rubbing alcohol (for racehorses), Night Nurse (5ml), Day Nurse (5ml), marmoset repellent, balsamic vinaigrette, cobra venom, quinoa, peyote, quinine, extract of Thresher shark, Earl Grey tea-bags. There were hundreds of ingredients below these, including Pimms numbers 1 through 7, Xylenium-16 (I Googled this one—turns out it's soviet-era experimental rocket fuel. Who knew?) A couple of hundred ingredients below the rocket fuel, we went headfirst down the rabbit hole after Alice, touching lightly on Boots No 7 pan stick foundation before crashing into Bill Brewer, Jan Stewer, Peter Gurney, Peter Davy, Dan'l Whiddon, Harry Hawke, Old Uncle Tom Cobley and all. I always woke in a cold sweat.

I even considered whether Katherine had caught malaria at Boots the Chemists' serving counter while buying cotton buds. Prickly heat (niacin flushing) had been tagged as a recurring issue, but absolutely every business builder in the community jumped to comment: This was normal. Harmless. A mere feeling of warmth in combination with some redness. Your skin might tingle, but the sensation would quickly pass. A story doing the rounds involving a woman from Reading whose prickly heat was a precursor to the spontaneous combustion of her Afro hairdo turned out to be an urban myth. Phew!

In fact, the only mention of hot flushes was from positive posts where some women previously subject to hot flushes claimed the products, once used, left them flush- free. It upset me, not finding a solution for Katherine, so we agreed that she would stop using one product at a time until we pinpointed the trouble-maker.

You see, what I did not realise at the time and foolishly never questioned, was why Katherine seemed to be the first victim of this affliction. It was an extremely active group; why had nobody picked up on this before? Maybe, they had. Can you guess the rest? Yep, the Admins heavily policed this issue. Remember, negative feedback acted like Kryptonite on the chances of fence-sitting prospects still within the group— which typically had not yet decided whether to invest or not. The delete button was frequently used—allegedly. This is pure speculation.

I had been at one time offered an Admin role because they needed somebody in the GMT zone, but there was no way I would be able to cope with the traffic on top of my full-time job, so I politely declined. I think they would probably have given me the bum's rush anyway because I would not kowtow to their rules. I lost the chance to go behind the scenes, but who cares. It would not have made me a better network marketer, though it might have made me resent MLM quicker.

Now hear this: Successful MLM professionals have thousands of people in their downline. How do they cope with people that have issues? How did they provide 5-star service? Yes, yes, they did what I'd been told to do—tag on posts and send links to the appropriate information on the company FAQ website. Still, potentially, you could spend your entire day (not 15 minutes a day!) addressing people's problems, and that could become a full-time job in itself.

Me! Me! Me!

I secretly yearned to reply: 'You've got problems! What about me, sister? I have attached a bulleted list of the top fifty ball-breakingly annoying things currently ganging up on me to stop me from getting rich. If you want to do something constructive, help me with those, instead of whining to me!'

Anyone considering career suicide in MLM should give this a try.

Regardless, I still found tagging and sending links to boiler plated documents too impersonal. Those people had invested money with you, and I felt responsible for them. Is this why I failed? Did I care too much?

Sigh

Sadly, Katherine's hot flushes remained a mystery. She accepted that it could be a pure coincidence because she was of an age when hot flushes were not out of the question. We continued to talk, but I found myself more and more engrossed in her fascinating life rather than plotting our plan to hit the road and organise market stalls, speak to gym owners and get our business off the ground.

Do you remember my fancy OneNote with all the information overload? Well, I shared that with her. After all, it was the bible to my MLM tribe, my team handover notes.

Katherine promised she'd take a look at it, but she probably never opened it. Who could blame her? I had dumped my entire collection on her the same way Simone dumped hers on me (Cue SFX of the Serious Miscalculation Siren at volume 11!)

Cringe

She got one friend interested enough to sign up as a customer. She invited her to the FB community, following the group's protocol. This 'friend' was hyperactive in the group, which was excellent—up to a point. That point was when she started posting bizarre comments and making stuff up.

I never understood this behaviour, but some people are compulsive liars or attention seekers. But how do you lie about something written in ink on page one of the book of startlingly obvious fibs? Hear this: The imminent launch of a new seasonal shake flavour on the US market evoked a frenzy in all biz builders as they fell over each other to pre-sell with massive hype because seasonal flavours only appeared a few times a year, of course. Otherwise, your only choice was three core flavours—Vanilla, Very Vanilla and Super Vanilla Plus (I made these flavours up, sorry)

The more hype you created, the larger quantities would sell, and more sales points converted to a bigger payday. Considering this 'friend' was from the UK market, she commented on one of the hype posts, 'Don't bother peeps, I tried this; it tastes shit.' That product hadn't even been released yet and was unlikely to be sold in the UK?! WTH?

Witch-finder General

Back end, angry exchanges erupted like an active volcano as a small army of keyboard Witchfinder Generals took holy orders, climbed into their crusader pants and rode abroad in search of the 'evil one'. This blackguard put this person in the group. Initially, people pointed accusatory fingers digits at Katherine. Then the crusaders discovered that I had encouraged this cuckoo into the MLM nest! In a labyrinthine version of the McCarthy purges, one by one, the dominoes fell in sequence. I led back to Anna, who Simone had added. So they made a beeline to Simone to get in touch with Katherine, to get in touch with her loopy friend to promptly have a word with her because they were deleting her comment.

Can you see the bureaucracy here? Why they could not private message the wacky friend themselves was beyond me, they had to create such a hoo-hah about it! I was not too fond of the way this had been dealt with.

Goodbye Katherine

After a few months, we drifted apart. I am not sure if it was because I was a crappy leader, or because Katherine's business at home was growing faster than an ice-lolly franchise during a July heatwave and eating up her time.

I use 'leader' loosely. Katherine was supposed to be my partner, but I had to take the lead in introducing her to this company. As a rough guide to the kind of leader I was, General George Custer at the Battle of the Little Big Horn would be a good fit (Final score: Crazy Horse et al., 1, The seventh cavalry, 0 after extra time.) Honestly, I was rubbish.

There was a damned good reason why I thrived in the autonomous roles I sought and occupied in my corporate career. First of all, I have no idea how to be a good leader, especially in a subject I am not an expert in, and I am not afraid to admit it. It is hard if you do not have a role model to imitate. I learn from experience and by observing others. I am not a theoretical person. If I were, I'd have come up with a theory on why mirrors reverse what they reflect from left to right and not from top to bottom (don't dwell on this, it'll hurt your head.)

To paraphrase Confucius, 'What you learn you forget, what you see you remember, what you do you understand.'

And if you understand, well, anything is possible.

So, just how wonderful and life-transforming are these shakes?
I dunno.

Chapter 16

BACK TO THE DRAWING BOARD, AND DON'T SPARE THE HORSES!

In which: Peggy revisits the drawing board — There are hard times ahead — Haters gonna hate, hate, hate, hate, hate! — Brutal postings emerge — Peggy contemplates the Spaghetti Hoops and Rhubarb Crumble diet — Our heroine feels like a dyspeptic boatman rowing his way across the Pentland Firth in a coracle

---

Randy

Back to the drawing board. What hadn't I done that others had done to gain success? Why wasn't my name a household name like Derek Worre (or whatever he calls himself nowadays.)

There must be a solution to this! Even the Rubik's Cube had an answer.

I formed a close friendship with a few ladies who, like me, were as deflated as the balloons after a 6th birthday party. They lived on the other side of the world but were of UK origin, ex-pats in Asia. Claire and Susan started MLM a couple of years before I did, and Shelly probably started a year after me. We used to participate in the same Zoom call every Sunday, and you could see that we had similar levels of frustration.

Then one day, I was put in a WhatsApp group and asked if I would like to be part of an exclusive sub-group. Hell yes! I was willing to try anything. At this point, I still believed I could ride to the penthouse at the top of the MLM escalator.

I just had not found a system that worked for me, so I was excited that they'd invited me to be part of their little group. Like me, they also followed anybody and everybody remotely successful on social media and one guy called Randy caught Claire's attention.

I believe Randy was still a few bucks shy of millionaire status; his cuff links were gold plated rather than solid 24 carat, but the way he was going, he was galloping down that glory road.

He freely advertised his 'system' on his Facebook profile. That way, he attracted new customers and business builders to his MLM opportunity. He also worked hard to attract struggling MLM reps because he was selling his system, mentoring you to success, using precisely the methods he used to gain his traction. This sounded pretty ginger-peachy to me because finally, I could see first-hand what successful leaders did daily instead of just reading about it.

We all agreed to buy his system and split the cost of the mentoring; Claire would front this. I think the total cost was around $500, so I paid approximately a hundred quid. Obviously, we did not tell him there were four of us paying for this because he would have felt cheated. But he was more than happy for Claire to share the system with her downline. And let's be honest, the only way to make good money in the organisation was if your team duplicated what you did and promoted to higher ranks.

Getting customers is more straightforward than getting business builders. Customers often have the stamina of an asthmatic tortoise, regularly failing to last beyond the first month. And who wants to chase new customers over hill and dale? Smart money enticed those interested in building the business because as their organisation grows, your organisation grows. Neither of us was in Claire's downline, but we were one team and trusted each other implicitly.

As sad as it was to be a founder member of Losers-R-Us (that's how it felt, anyway), it was refreshing to hear each other's stories on the rocky MLM journey so far. We encouraged and cheered each other on, exchanged tips, discussed obstacles, shared our frustrations and were there for each other when needed.

After payment, Claire arranged a one-to-one session with Randy. She wanted to make sure that we got the same benefit from it as she would've, so she recorded the conversation for us. Sneaky, right? But when you are hungry to succeed, rules are more straightforward to bend than a wet flannel.

'For Sale' groups

By this point, I was as disappointed as a woman who opens the biscuit barrel expecting to find a Cherry Bakewell for her elevenses, only to discover that her children have scoffed every last one (based on a true story). The system had soared to a new level of cringe. My heart sank faster than a bowling ball in quicksand. I hoped for a different outcome against my better judgement. Still, once I heard the recorded session, my worst suspicions were confirmed: Posting in FB 'For Sale' groups was a bigger no-no than attending an AGM wearing a Mexican poncho and spurs.

Listen to this, though; this guy recruited like 25 new people in the past month alone, the same amount of people I attracted to my business in 18 months! He must be doing something right!

All for one and one for all!

I decided that now was the time to up gear, get out there and make it work. To hit that turbo-booster. If not now, when? Besides, we had made a Three Musketeers type pact: One for all, and all for one! We were in it together (up to our necks?), and nothing could stop us.

Have you ever posted anything to a public Facebook group? They're not hard to find. Every city, town and hamlet has one. It's usual to see one for chit-chat and another, which is like an online marketplace where people sell anything from the Tower Bridge (watch out for this one, it's a scam) to a single sock.

And these were the groups he wanted us to target. The idea was to join as many groups as I possibly could—especially those that have at least 5,000 members and looked active based on how many daily posts you could see.

You needed to read all the group rules before you hit join because several of these groups were thoughtful about the ninja tactics of MLM sensei. If you discovered anything that sounded like 'no self-promotion, no direct selling' or similar, joining these groups was as much use as a 100 Watt bulb to a blind man.

Before and after

We each kept a spreadsheet with the groups we'd requested to join and the relevant dates. Once approved, we would start posting. Randy gave us about 15 pre-written posts with before and after pictures of amazing transformations from reps and customers, which he found to be the most successful in terms of engagement. All we had to do was to copy and paste. Easy, right? We had a full script of what to say when people commented. Again, pretty much a case of—if I may quote Oscar Wilde here: 'Easy-peasy Lemon-Squeezy.'

Wrong! Wrong with bells on! And a red ribbon on top. Doh'! It turned out to be as easy as folding an origami camel whilst wearing snow mittens. I had made a classic grammatical blunder, confusing 'being easy' with 'making it sound easy'.

Anyone interested in your post never worked off a script—certainly not mine as it turned out—when asking questions. Each had unique needs and asked questions in random order. I tried to find answers that fitted and then get back on track. Hopeless. I have never felt more uncomfortable.

My spreadsheet with approved groups blossomed. I started with the larger cities, then opened google maps and just found some smaller towns, popped it in the group search on FB, read the rules, hit join, and added my spreadsheet 'awaiting approval'.

In this part of the system, I was super-efficient. I was already part of these groups in my own and surrounding towns, but my intention was never to post there. However, the leadership's advice had always been to become known as the 'shake lady' because word of mouth recommendations happen, and I needed to be at the forefront of their mind.

Perhaps a gardening analogy might help here. Imagine you are asked if you knew somebody who could cut your hedge. You give them the name of a person you know cuts hedges—same scenario. Somebody might be looking into protein shakes, and instantly, you pop in their mind, and they recommend you. Or you hoped so! It would be best if you became known in your town for what you promote. We all know who does 'Avon' in our village, for example. Also, on these groups, people often asked, 'Who on here does The Body Shop'?

But I had no desire to become the 'shake lady'. The title was too close to 'snake lady', and I did not want to spend the rest of my life living down a name that made me sound like a sexual deviant.

The part where you start posting in these groups was brutal. Like, ten times worse than I anticipated. Despite the negativity and rudeness, it was also highly entertaining, and I had ten times as many conversations as before. I created a spreadsheet with all the people that commented on my post, and I contacted them via private message.

I kept track of what emojis they used to react to my post (sad, I know) and to which group they belonged (significant detail). I kept a record of their reasons for using the products: was it weight loss, lack of energy or overall health? So I could have more meaningful conversations with them. Otherwise, I would lose track. I could extract 15 keen prospects and 25 haters calling me a scammer or worse from one post.

Some of the haters displayed unique traits that set them truly apart from the rest of humanity. For one thing, they had the cunning and guile of a mollusc (there are a lot of molluscs to choose from, but I favour the limpet). By this, I mean they were too stupid to know how profoundly stupid they were.

They'd post comments about before and after publicity shots, like:

'You can't fool me, the first picture's a bloke, and the second's a transvestite.' Or vice versa. Or,

'Lol! So the woman in the second photo suddenly got a tattoo of the nine-horned beast on her forehead, did she?'

You knew they were drawing from the same deep well of ignorance they'd been drawing buckets from since their days in primary six.

Still, undaunted, I turned to the wisdom of the ancients with a 'Bless—Release—Delete'. I would go straight to their profile and instantly block them. This would stop them snooping around my Facebook page. It was human nature to check the profiles of others. These people could turn into stalkers because they had nothing better to do than bully others. So, the sooner I blocked them, the less the impact of their spit-speckled, ranting hatred.

This was where the support groups earned their keep. Regularly swapping our funny and not-so-funny stories with Claire, Susan, and Shelly, made me realise that this was happening to all of us. We exchanged the names of the worst offenders so my colleagues could block these horrible individuals too. We got smarter the more we posted into groups. We'd search to see for existing posts about weight loss, pounds, kilos, or anything similar to our stuff. If we did, we would read through the comments, find the bad guys and block them in advance.

To start with, we posted once a week because sometimes there were many prospects to follow up, and with a full-time job (by now, you probably think that I am constantly using this as an excuse), it was not practical to converse with them during the day. Randy told us the optimal time to post was 8 AM, but the problem was, if you post at that time and can't get to the post until 4 PM due to work, you'd have no idea what was happening. Besides, unadorned hatred always outweighs positive interest, which made you dread going back to it. Anyway, most people work during the day and those that did not have anything better to do than give random strangers grief.

Some of the ladies in our little circle preferred not to check back during the day, but I had to. I had to block all the haters asap. Others had two FB accounts to ensure that the account they used for posting wasn't precious to them. This stood in stark contrast to mine, which had pictures of my kids from infancy.

I, no exaggeration, lived in fear of the outcome of these posts (what if, in my absence, a voodoo priestess were to cast a spell on me, transforming me into a zombie, lurching around like a punk rocker on his fifteenth pint of Newcastle Brown at a Sex Pistols' concert? Eh? What then? Just saying.)

Sometimes I didn't get any traction at all. I might as well have deleted the post, made a note on my spreadsheet that this group was as dead as Monty Python's iconic parrot, removed myself from the group and moved on to the next one.

The plan was to find groups with high engagement levels because you would return to the same group over time to post again. Randy said he had five groups that he posted regularly; he was confident there were enough members who may not have seen his post the last time and may show interest the next time. He posted daily, and he knew his script inside out. His lovely wife partnered with him, and both did MLM as full-time careers, so they had a system where one posted while the other connected with prospects. Good teamwork.

After a few months of posting and feeling more nauseous than a dyspeptic boatman rowing his way across the Pentland Firth in a coracle, I decided to throw in the towel. I could no longer face exposing genuine people that had experienced excellent results from the products to the knuckle-dragging morons (and that's letting some of them off lightly) who would gratuitously insult them without their knowledge.

Their pictures were shared with consent. We never stole them from their private FB profiles. When you posted in groups, you consented to share the content unless you specifically opted not to. There were also groups specifically for sharing before and after pictures due to our products, so we should never run out.

There were instances of highly unethical behaviour. Some people would steal progress pictures from someone on social media, promoting a different product! For example, they might steal before-and-after snaps of someone who'd been following the Spaghetti Hoops and Rhubarb Crumble diet for eighteen months and use them as examples of their diet's success!

Out of about one hundred conversations I had on messenger, only one prospect was willing to talk to me on the phone, then cancelled half an hour before we were due to speak. I added no more than five people to the large FB community. They were the nosey curtain twitcher types who planned to sit with a fence post up the crack of their butts for a little longer. Very few accepted my friend requests.

By now, I felt as if I had nothing left to give. All my options had been exhausted, and I seriously considered jacking the whole thing in. My dream of building a private label product remained very much alive, and I hated myself for getting distracted with MLM instead of focussing on the one thing that I wanted the most. But when a carrot-dangler breezes into town, dangling carrots, fanning the embers of your dreams, rekindling the idea of firing your boss on your way to financial freedom, surely you can forgive me for being naïve as those hapless apprentices. They shuffled off to the company store, searching for a left-handed screwdriver and a litre of tartan paint.

Chapter 17

MLM: THE GOOD, THE BAD AND THE 'GOOD HEAVENS, DID A TREE FALL ON YOU?'

In which: Self-discovery and self-learning flourish — Peggy loses 20 pounds in 90 days — Peggy sets her sights on working once, getting paid for eternity — 100% belief, 130% effort equals top 1 percent; the arithmetic of MLM!

They say that life is what wrecks your plans once you've made them. My life as an MLM professional was slowly coming to an end. Shock. Horror. I did not end up richer than Bill Gates' wealth manager, financially unchained or livin La Vida Loca as I followed the jet set around the planet.

Nor did I raise money for my private label product inventory as I intended. I ended up defeated and frustrated, and wallowing in credit card debt up to the underwire in my bra.

I had 18 wonderful months feeling extremely healthy and happy with my overall health. I was leaner than a racing snake, my skin glowed like the Cleopatra of legend. I felt younger than my years. But as with any diet regime, if you do not keep it up, you do not get to keep it.

I sustained a knee injury, so my normal exercise routine went out of the window. As with many diets when this happens, my healthy eating habits jumped out the same window and chased it down the street. As is often the way with diet Karma, I piled back on all the weight I'd lost—and a smidge more in my final 6 months (now that's a twist of the knife!) So not only did

I end up skint, but my scales displayed a daily record of my shameful recidivism when I climbed out of the shower.

But let's not dwell on that, let me take this opportunity to reflect on the two years of my MLM journey, starting with the good stuff.

The Good - Community

I really tuned in to self-development and personal growth during my redundancy process. I was again exposed to this during my attempts to become the next MLM professional. There is no doubt that I was positively influenced into self-discovery and self-learning. Every event I attended and every book that was recommended to me fuelled the desire in me to be a better person and to do good in the world. 'Focus on positivity. Start the day on a positive note. Practise gratitude.' There is so much we can be grateful for.

Sure, we always want more. But stop for a moment to think about how much you have, and I am pretty sure you'll see it is a hell of a lot more than millions of other people out there. Those little things have a major impact on the way you live your life. Your outlook on life changes when you embark on a personal development journey.

The great thing about network marketing was the sense of community. The UK market consisted of a friendly bunch of people cheering you on, people that genuinely cared and wanted you to succeed. They were happy to share their material, they organised mass 'introduction party presentations' by hiring function rooms in fancy bars in Manchester and invited all the associates that were interested in attending.

All they asked, was for you to confirm attendance, bring your prospects along and they would do the rest. They may have asked you to pay a fiver to cover a flute of Prosecco for the guests on arrival, but those were small potatoes considering they did all the selling for you. Kind, right? They had nothing to gain.

They weren't benefiting from any of us 'strangers' signing our prospects into our organisation. If you think about it, those gatherings were genius, they demonstrated professionalism and the more people were in the room, the less awkward your prospects felt, because they were not the only ones looking at this opportunity. Compare it to my failed 'home party events' with zero attendees! Yeah, exactly! I planned to bring Katherine to one of these meetings, so she could see the culture and meet other people, but it wasn't meant to be.

Of course, every MLM company is unique as is every geographical location. Interestingly, I had a somewhat different impression from the US and Asia teams. One that I loosely belonged to. I never felt part of their community, but let me save that for the other chapter, we are discussing the good stuff here.

Being part of a great community means you get to meet a variety of new people some of whom became friends for life. You accumulated plenty of acquaintances, but there are few people in my friends list that I would consider friends and there is no way we would ever have crossed paths had we not been in the same MLM company.

The Good - Templates

There is no doubt about the massive efforts made by head office to educate the reps. They streamlined and bullet-proofed our system to facilitate easy duplication from associates to their prospects. You literally had to follow the system, and teach your prospect the same system, so that your prospect could teach their prospect the same system. You get the gist. Keep it simple. Templates are great—If you agree with them.

I signed up about a year after my MLM company entered the UK market, and unfortunately many templates were still using 'American' jargon, which, personally, I found really hard to use. The same was true for the templates and information I inherited from Simone because we fell under the US/Asia team that had grown over time. The UK was very much virgin territory at the time and few associates came from the UK, so they had no need to change it.

They told me I could rewrite the scripts if I didn't feel they were appropriate, but as a newbie network marketer, I could have done with a little more help from the team, considering the Asia leaders were UK expats.

Thankfully, the head office took a proactive stance and listened to its UK associates, and over time, these templates were rewritten to better fit the British business culture. They were brilliant at it, always happy to help. They manned phones, responded to emails promptly, treated us with lots of respect, participated in Q&A sessions in the company FB community and to cap it all a nicer bunch of people you couldn't hope to meet. We met many of them at the organised events and celebrations. I genuinely appreciate what they did for us.

Some high achievers often created their own system and templates that worked for them and their team and they were only too happy to share it with a wider audience, so you were spoilt for choice.

Being part of many different support groups, messenger and WhatsApp groups was another wonderful way to learn, receive encouragement and feel included.

The Good - Products

Because the products worked, we were never short of success stories. This encouraged the people you had invited to the FB community because people loved to brag about every pound and inch they lost.

And when you had somebody on the fence, who could not decide if it were worth the money, seeing results they were jealous of, they could more easily be swayed to buy.

I was one of the success stories. In 90 days, I lost 20 pounds and I looked fit. I know, ('rolling eyes') nothing like self-praise, but I was forty years old and felt seriously good in my own skin. I bought a gig on Fiverr and had my transformation turned into a little video. It was witty, educational and a real deal. It was popular in the groups I shared it in. And not the brutal-for-sale groups, but the private Facebook communities with prospects.

I was even asked for consent to allow some associates to share it with their team groups. I had no issue with it, because I was proud. I just prayed that it would never fall under the public's pitiless gaze. Worse still, what if some keyboard warrior with a grudge or a small penis, vented his spleen by uploading my stuff to the dark web! They say the dark web's full of drug-smugglers, arms-runner, conspiracy theorists and Avon reps. God knows what they'd do with my video.

The products contained only premium-quality 100% natural ingredients: No artificial sweeteners, no soy, no GMOS, no gluten, just pure, organic goodness. They never had the organic stamp and you had to believe them with the other claims, but I had no reason for doubt.

The full system, including supplements, was revolutionary. Weight loss was not the primary selling point, it was a health system which was designed to bring your body back into balance, improve mental focus, body composition through fat loss, improve sleep and give your body the nutrition lacking in today's foods. They said our food was nutritionally bankrupt due to depleted soil. The standard white bread you'd find nowadays on any supermarket shelf is made from wheat out of which all vestige of nutrition has been summarily thrashed before baking.

The Good - Environment

The company sources their ingredients from the most natural places on earth. Products were tested for heavy metals, pesticides, herbicides, and other nasty stuff you'd rather not find in a shake, to ensure only the best quality products reached the customer.

The company is environmentally responsible and has a bold ambition to achieve zero waste by 2023. They package many of their products in post-consumer recycled plastic. And they use solar panels to generate renewable energy. The company donates money to non-profit organisations. An Earth, Wind and Fire concert could not have produced more positive vibes.

The Good - Money

'Work once, get paid for eternity.'

I sort of agree with this. If you put the work in, 100% believe in the product, the company, the business model and in yourself, you will end up in the top 1%, and will reap in the benefits of passive income.

One thing puzzled me. The company is not yet 20 years old yet there was much talk about leaving a legacy behind. Your children were to inherit your MLM organisation. They'd be set for life? Was there any truth in this legacy malarkey? I found it hard to believe. I could conjure up no one who might be described as 'second generation' in any network marketing company I knew of. I'm not looking to dispute the claim outright, but you just have to consider traditional businesses—they often go bust and there's nothing to inherit, no legacy left behind. Google how many MLM companies have gone into administration. Just saying.

Regardless of the long-term vision, there's good money to be had. You could hire a manservant whose only role was to keep you supplied with watermelon scented Turkish delight if that's what floats your boat. Travel to exotic places in a hot-air balloon (heaven knew there was enough hot air in MLM to waft you to the far flung corners of the globe.) If you were willing to work for it, you could have what your heart desired.

I can absolutely see the money rolling in if you lead a team of hungry, passionate associates who catch the same vision as you and together you can expand your business until it rivals the soon to be trillion-dollar Apple brand.

As the legendary singer, Tom Jones very nearly said: 'MLM dosh is like candy on a shelf. Just reach right up and help yourself!' There are more ways to pay you than the government has of taxing it back off you again. Daily and weekly paydays, monthly bonuses, competitions to exciting destinations and many more additional incentives. Obviously, I am not in pole position to tell you about these, because I did not belong to the elite 1%, but I know they exist. No hard feelings.

The beautiful thing about the mandatory monthly investment needed to stay active, and participate in the compensation plan, is your actual grocery shopping. You basically eat your overhead.

Sounds awesome, right? Don't think that protein shakes are your only option. You can have energy and performance products, supplements, or if you are in the demographic market where they sell beauty products, well, you do whatever suits you best.

Many reps keep in tip top condition and consume the system daily, post like crazy on social media to prove how easy the system works. Basically, you use what you buy, with no need to buy stock and then flog it. An attractive proposition. The amount of MLM companies that force you to invest in upfront inventory or get samples is ridiculous. That's all well and good, just be vigilant—Spend enough on your products to accumulate the required monthly points, otherwise you slip into (Cue theatrical thunder and lightning effects)—'Inactive' status!

Achieve this dubious category and wave bye-bye to your hard-earned moolah. It is as easy to do as to avoid. So, keep your wits about you.

Chapter 18

THE BAD: BRAINS WASHED WHILE YOU WAIT

In which: Brainwashing is considered wrong and bad — The bigger the why, the more effortless the how; the linguistics of MLM — The 'but' is shrunk — Toxic Positivity rears its head — Inherited MLM empires: Urban myth or golden legacy? The Good, the Bad and the Ugly; the three faces of MLM.

The Bad - Community

I will start with the community because I already mentioned it largely depends on demographic location. Besides, the idea of community wasn't what sold MLM to me. I am a very neutral person, and I have always been everybody's friend (almost everybody's; I wasn't keen on General Ghaddafi when he was around.)

Deep down, I suppose I am a one-to-one person. I have one best friend from primary school, one best friend from secondary school, one husband, (ok maybe I've gone overboard with two kids), and I carried this pattern throughout my whole life.

Thumbs up to gatherings, thumbs down to crowds. I feel more comfortable with fewer people around. I am as loyal as a rescued Elkhound puppy, and I am all for quality over quantity. I do not like pretend friends. To those who do not add value to my life, I say: 'Pick your window; you're leaving!'

This is one of the reasons why I thrive in autonomous roles. Yet this may be the self-same reason for the crash and burning of my network marketing career! It's all part of the Instant-Karma, instant-noodle lifestyle we all lead now—part of the Hare Krishna, Harry Ramsden, Ying-Yang (or should that be the Ding-Dong) of the universe that eastern mystics are always (quite literally) banging their drums about?

I enjoyed all the events and coaching. Self-development was valuable. But brainwashing was just wrong and bad. And lots of the training was pure brainwashing. Of course, nobody called it that, but it was happening.

I even tried to brainwash myself. I could never remember the essential script to explain the compensation plan. You were supposed to know it word for word, and if the situation calls for you to speak to a prospect when you are out and about, you should be able to recite it as you drew it on the back of a napkin: 'Repetition is the mother of all skills.'

It wasn't complicated, yet I had to try so hard to remember it. I decided the only way to learn it was to do what Bart Simpson had to do after class and write it out a hundred times. Did it help? No. I typed it up 3 or 4 times each day for about six months, and I was still making mistakes. Destiny did not intend me to learn it. Tut, utter thicko.

All MLM communities are full of encouraging mottos with persuasive charm. I could bury you in these. I still have them on my phone, but here is just a little taster:

'The bigger your WHY, the easier your HOW!'

'When you argue for your limitations, you get to keep them.'

'I don't sell stuff. I offer hope, health, excitement, and freedom. I lock arms with people who want to do the same and have fun doing it.'

'If you want to reach your goals, you must shrink the size of your BUT.'

'Don't wait for the perfect moment; take the moment and make it perfect.'

'It's not just the weight you lose but the life you gain.'

'Your only limit is YOU.'

'You can't have a million-dollar dream with a minimum wage work ethic.'

You get the gist. Or would you call those clichés? Why pussyfoot around? It's plain and straightforward preaching!

The Bad - Products

Vague was always in vogue in the MLM world. The airy-fairy-ness was necessary to create hype and curiosity. This was bloody annoying and as transparent as a politician's promise. I hated their assumption that powdered food was the only foundation of an acceptable lifestyle. Those partial to a weekend McDonald's Happy Meal were scowled at with the same intensity as witches in mediaeval Europe. And the condescending posts: 'Are you sure you know what's in it?' Sheesh!

Again I summoned up my inner Ms Marbles of Agatha Crispy fame and ran an eagle's eye over the ingredients list of our main selling product. I counted fifty, of which I recognised maybe ten. The rest might as well have been written backwards in Paraguay's Guarani dialect for all the sense I could make of them. Some of the elements weren't even in the periodic table!

The brass-neckery of it. How could you call this a nutritional meal when you genuinely did not understand what was in it? How could you compare that to a beef burger made from 100% British beef?! These berating posts about what people ate were supposed to be educational. After all, 'This is the reason why people come to your social media page!'

'Roll eyes. Roll drums. ROFLOL!'

Do you want to know the cynical truth about why people from your MLM come to your wall to like and comment on something cringy? It's because they want you to reciprocate. None of my friends ever liked anything related to MLM, but the moment I posted a joke or anything genuine, the comments section and emojis exploded on that post. This just told me that they chose to ignore the MLM posts, cringe and scroll past as fast as their mouse could help them do so.

I'm holding my hands out. Cuff me. Take me 'downtown' and 'book me' if that's how policemen speak nowadays. I posted some educational crap on my wall. The bulk of it oozed positivity, courage, inspiration and exercise, nothing patronising because I have morals. Or did I. But what if I was wrong? The brainwashed do not have self-awareness. They think they're doing good, and all the while, they behave like muppets.

Back in year zero, when I first walked, wide-eyed, into the MLM Emporium of Wonder and Promise, when I was still chasing down financial and time freedom, I was motivated. It was easy to post. Now that I have washed my hands of MLM, it is fun to see these Facebook memories pop up daily. It's my turn to preach to myself. And by the way, here's a question worth asking—shouldn't a multi-billion dollar company claiming 'organic' stature for products be capable of having that fact certified?

The Bad - Toxic positivity

Everything you post has to be positive. Everything you do must be positive. Did you know that there is such a thing as toxic positivity? Sounds peculiar, right? 'Toxic and Positivity' don't look right snuggled down together in the same sentence. Like 'Non-alcoholic lager' or 'Socially distanced wrestling.'

Now, listen up, because this is important. Toxic positivity is the culture of portraying yourself as being happy no matter what. You're disengaged from anything that might seem remotely negative. It's a close relative of the idea of encouraging people always to see the bright side, never to open up about anything bad.

Trying to stay positive in your role of Jolly Lady Boss, when you are pretty sure you could cry continuously until the following Monday, requires Herculean effort. I am not a close pal of Negative Nancy (13, Gloomy Mansions, Dullsville), but we all have our moments.

I've never made money or broken even, but I was always smart enough to keep my full-time job. That way, 'losses' weren't as noticeable because I had a salary coming in. But you heard horror stories about people who'd lost far more than money—although they lost that too in truckloads: friends, dignity, and marriages all suffered irreparable damage. Some things cannot be hidden. If people know you in person, they will know that your social media persona is a whopping big lie. Please don't 'fake it until you make it', I beg you. People will see through you.

You were sold the oldest desirable commodities in history: hopes and dreams. Your community encouraged you when, in fact, they were guilt-tripping you. And if it did not work out, only one person would be left carrying the responsibility stick—you!

'You didn't work hard.'

'You didn't contact enough people.'

'You didn't listen to your mentor.'

'You didn't surround yourself with the right people.'

'You didn't'……fill in the blanks.

Your community were never more than acquaintances. Fake friends. Is that what you want?

The Bad - Sacrifice

One particular story of 'sacrifice' will never leave me, not least because it reaches new heights of cringe. It's a distressing tale of cult behaviour and the brainwashed mentality.

It saddens me that this story was told to me with pride and conviction of its moral correctness.

Sigh

Emily was fast becoming one of the UK's elite consultants in our company, so she was asked to share her story and do some coaching on stage in front of hundreds of consultants. Emily started with preaching work ethic and what it takes to be successful in this business.

This was standard fare in MLM circles. Talk to everybody, from supermarket cashiers to the waitress who fetched your coffee or the guy waiting at the bus stop. Any sentient creature with a pulse was fair game for sharing your story. You never knew Emily said who needed to hear your story!

That said, you need to hear Emily's story to grasp a significant point about the darker implementations of MLM. Up to this point, I have tried to keep my promise to you to entertain and inform. However, though indispensable to my exploration of MLM, Emily's story is undeserving of any comic spin. So put your serious face on for a couple of minutes until I spill the beans. I'll let you know when to put your happy face back on.

Emily's Story

Emily said that the second most important activity was the launch party. For me, even thinking about this got me so worked up I had to stick my head down the toilet bowl and flush to calm me down. She said she intended to host a party and that there'd be several 'strangers' there in her living room.

This was all run-of-the-mill fare. However, while in full sales mode, Emily received devastating news: her teenage daughter had made a suicide attempt and was now in hospital.

How would you react when faced with such news? Get hysterical? Collapse? It's hard to say. Everybody's different—well, Emily certainly was, because the first thing she said was, 'You gotta do what you gotta do, folks.' And went on, without a break, to finish her presentation. After all, these lovely people had all come to hear about her 'wonderful opportunity.'

I froze, traumatised by the thought that Emily would raise the mighty dollar above her only child's wellbeing. Her body language demanded recognition of her loyalty and commitment to the company.

I want to think that nobody—nobody I knew anyway, that's for sure—would take inspiration from Emily's misguided reaction; that the most common emotional response would be disgust. Yet some—it could only have been the brainwashed—clapped their approval.

I tried not to climb on my high horse over this. After all, I, too, had made family sacrifices, though none involved life or death decision making. Neither had I ever lost a friend through my MLM participation (Many MLM leaders preached that we should expect to lose friends and even embrace the fact. 'It's their loss, not yours,' they'd sneer, 'They're jealous. What kind of friend refuses to cheer you on?')

(Call To Action: Remove your serious face and put your happy face on.)

I still thank my lucky stars that my friends stuck with me during my lunatic phase of thinking there were indeed three steps to heaven; the first drinking shakes, the second selling shakes, and the third, trying to keep your head above water in a sea of passive income.

I'm grateful too that I didn't hornswoggle (Look it up if you must, but it's precisely the right word) anybody I knew. If I had only hornswoggled a few, perhaps the mighty Passive Income River would have burst its banks, and we'd all have drowned in greenbacks. But I think that I was going to lose interest regardless. After all, I lack the social extrovert's ability to spontaneously strike up a meaningful conversation with a stranger at the Waitrose deli counter on the fascinating subject of the weight loss plateau.

I got to a point with events where I was as enthusiastic as an atheist singing in a tabernacle choir. Nothing surprised me anymore. I knew what they were going to present and preach. It was like watching the same less-than-hilarious stand-up comic's act for the fifteenth time.

Twice, my birthday fell on an event or a celebration—rotten luck. The first time, in London. A weekend event. We went to Pizza Express with some of the team for dinner. But it was not a celebration; it was just dinner because some people were starving. At one point, I thought that if the Roast Pumpkin and Chorizo (with extra mushrooms) didn't reach our table soon, some of us might start eating the napkins. Some of them had, but I'm not naming names (Not me, of course, I had my appetite well under control.)

In my second year, I attended another two-day event in Manchester, which was closer to home. I booked a hotel for four people, so my husband and kids came on the train, and we all went to a nice Teppanyaki restaurant in the evening, I remember it well because although they had lashings of Teppans, there was 'a bit of a hold up in the Yaki supply chain' (a Brexit thing, they said)—we got an apology and a 10% discount.

I was supposed to return for the second day of the event on Sunday but decided to go home with my family. I felt the shame as intensely as a middle-aged, normally sober woman the morning after the night before her office party, remembering how she'd mooned the minister of her local church from the upper deck of a number 47 bus as she made her drunken journey home. Even that industrial level of embarrassment failed to make me sit through another day of lectures. With hindsight, I saw this as a tipping point, an omen almost. My MLM train was headed for the buffers.

The Bad - Social Media

Whoa! Where do I start?! Do you remember when they lured you in with their vision of MLM's sunlit uplands? Let's break the dream down for unbelievers, shall we?

- Uncapped residual income (I'll have some of that, please!)
- Location-independent (..and a large slice of that...)
- Flexible schedule (Include me in, sister!)
- Low risk – high reward (Praise the Lord!)
- Run sophisticated side gigs from your mobile phone (Yes, Yes, YES!)

Now that every man, woman, child, dog, cat, goldfish and prisoner detained at Her Majesty's pleasure has a smartphone, this had to be as easy as shelling peas. No office needed, no need to buy any additional equipment; everything you already have is everything you need to be successful.

Do the work once and get paid over and over. Easy peasy, Lemon Squeezy, like the man said. The biggest fib since President Nixon pleaded not guilty at Watergate. The harsh reality was that you got the customer signed up, and before the month was over, they'd buckled at the knees—wimps!

Sometimes they'd manage an entire month and then throw in the dishtowel. If I remember my school physics, this is Newton's fifth law: 'You can't get paid over and over by somebody that never reorders.'

I never knew that customer retention was such a massive concern and an ever-present one. The steady haemorrhaging of customers, just like the time your grandmother came home from the annual bowling club dance sporting a love bite, was never spoken of in polite company. Pity, because looking the other way on this issue facilitated a bigger illusion than the Indian rope trick.

It conferred bragging rights to the 'my tree's bigger than your tree' brigade, who boasted about having hundreds, even thousands of customers. While this was often technically true, in practice, it was deceptive nonsense. Why? Because these figures failed to exclude the multitude of inactive customers who had left the organisation. I heard rumours at the time that one big-tree boaster laid claim to fifty-six customers who, according to Wikipedia, perished during the Siege of Stalingrad.

I was naïve enough to think that once people signed up, committed, they stayed, and I would continue to reap the benefit of their reorders in perpetuity. I shared Dale Winton's sentiments when he said; 'you've got to be in it to win it!' But they weren't in it, not for the long haul like me. What a fool!

When you join MLM, you are told everything except the truth. So you keep on recruiting and connecting, aiming to talk to ten new people every single day. Because by the time you get your next 'yes', you can guarantee that you'll have lost a few customers from not so long ago. I genuinely believed that my customer base would grow steadily, whereas, in reality, you are fighting to keep people on board for as long as possible and keep networking in the meantime. This is as easy to manage as reconstructing the Taj Mahal in Minecraft.

I found it surprising how much effort even the prominent leaders were putting in to connect with new people daily. I did not think they needed to. Indeed after five years in business, earning six figures a year, you can afford to put your feet up? Or at least one foot up (is that even possible?)

Again, please excuse my utter idiocy; I did not have a clue. Or I was not educated by my upline? Whatever the reason, I was undoubtedly uneducated because they talk to you in riddles (what's got four legs and flies? Two pairs of trousers!) We got partial info that you had to decipher yourself. You couldn't have cracked it using an Enigma Machine. I know I'd signed up for time and financial freedom, working from my phone. But that couldn't mean clamping my smartphone to the side of my face with a carpenter's vice from dawn until dusk. Drop the depth charge of a full-time job into the mix, and you'd be lucky to have enough time leftover in which to sleep.

On one occasion, the leader on the stage shared the story of how her daughter told her, 'Mummy, I think you are all liars. You say that you are in this business to spend more time with your children and family. But all you do is spend time on your phone.'

That's how I felt. I was terrified I'd miss the one comment, message, post, remark, like or reply that might unlock the door to financial mastery. It had become an obsession. The leader went on to say that we must all improve our time management skills. She did not elaborate. It was a trade secret discussed in one of the Friday night's sessions with exceptional trainer Richard and not for the likes of us losers, but her unspecified improvement did not seem to involve a reduction in hours. Funny that!

The bold fact is: There are no shortcuts. If you want to know about shortcuts, do the Knowledge and become a London Cabby. It's called network marketing for a reason: If you aren't networking, you aren't winning.

You need to focus on one, at a stretch, two, social media platforms. Admittedly, the leaders were against tackling many different platforms at the same time. Well, at least in my MLM. In my case, this advice fell on deaf ears. Several leaders proved successful on different platforms, leaving me feeling (dramatic cue roll on the timpani) the full force of the FOMO!!

So you get yourself an account and try to juggle them all. You don't have a deep knowledge of individual social media platforms because each has a different algorithm, demographic audience, and purpose. If you post for presence alone, this will be as effective as hanging out your weekly wash during a sandstorm.

Several gurus, mentors, swamis, MLM Maharajahs, and Grand Poobah's are more than willing to induct you into the dark arts of social media. My advice: If you aren't making money, and you are in the red because you have to stay active, avoid enlisting an MLM Guru for support. Instead, track down a successful, inspiring person in your organisation, follow or befriend them on social media, then observe and learn.

Earlier, I touched on the number of private groups that have to be part of. It's ridiculous to keep track of them. It would be easier to keep a bee as a pet and follow that around (good luck with that one) because they expect you to participate in any you accept actively. This adds to the other stuff you need to do on your bloody phone (the one clamped to the side of your face with a carpenter's vice.)

Like pakora in an Indian restaurant, that's just for starters. There's the 'for sale' public groups where you 'advertise' to contend with too. I got in the habit of leaving my post for no more than 24 hours and then deleted it because I needed more haters and blockers like I needed a beehive hairdo.

We knew Randy left his posts in the group; we could search Facebook and confirm that he put his money where his sweet-talking mouth was. He has had many historical posts. But he had skin tougher than buffalo hide; he cut his teeth on facing down negativity and haters, whereas I did not have the stomach for it. Yes, I lost potential prospects, but I was losing sleep at night, and it wasn't worth it.

The Bad - Anti-MLM communities

Did you know that there are anti-MLM Facebook groups too? You'll want to keep an eye on those too—both eyes if you can manage it. They are mainly public, so you don't have to join to see the posts. Despite that, I would rather sign up for a course of monthly colonic irrigation sessions than join one of these fellows. The company's admin Sergeant will take one glance at your profile over the top of their steel-rimmed spectacles before ripping you a new one. When that's done, and you've been reduced to a gibbering shadow of your former self, they might just let you join.

These groups are for hardcore haters of MLM and angry ex-MLM reps bemoaning how the big, bad MLM bogey man never gave them a chance they deserved. But for nastiness to rival the Child Catcher from Chitty Chitty Bang Bang's nastier big brother, watch out for the copying and pasting of your posts and private messages for others to laugh at you and degrade you in public.

And whilst we are on the subject of haters, you might want to check out YouTube; that's where you'll find the crack troops of the anti-MLM army. They are capable of besieging MLM transgressors until they capitulate. You'll tune in one night to find yourself starring in somebody else's YouTube channel. But it won't be to praise your enthusiasm or promote your product. I have nothing against those channels, their sole aim is to expose, protect and educate naïve souls.

The main point here is to highlight the extent to which you'll need to be as vigilant as a nesting hawk to make sure your name doesn't get dragged through the mud. If you are the 'walk-past- dead-bodies-to-get-to-the-top type, you should be concerned, minion reps never feature.

Besides minding your own business, being proactive and supporting your teammates 24/7, you were also part of the private groups on Messenger and WhatsApp with patronising leaders who demanded you visit their posts to comment, like or share. One particular leader that was as many layers above me in my upline as the gods of Mount Olympus were above the apprentice goatherds of Ancient Greece called out her teammates. This she did by tagging them in the message so they'd get a notification and were duty-bound to go and do what they'd been ordered to do within a given timeframe.

Cringe

The Bad - Ghastly Templates

The ghastly templates were as annoying as the twittering budgerigar you 'bought' from a bloke down the Frog & Toad for a half-pint of Guinness. They should have made your life easier, but they didn't. I hated the scripts so much; I could never learn to recite them; I couldn't even remember my 30-second story. My story!

The bits I remembered sounded rehearsed, and when I veered 'off-road', losing the thread altogether, I couldn't improvise. It was the biggest disaster since the BBC gave Terry Wogan a record contract. I found scripts to be more of a burden than a boon. Yet they sell it to you like they'd done everything for you. All you had to do was remember it.

The Bad - Referrals

I agree with referrals in principle because word of mouth is always the best advertisement. I would disagree in practice, though—especially if I had to ask for referrals! Here's how it works. If you get a 'no' from your prospect, you simply ask them if they know somebody else who would be interested in your product or opportunity. Worse still, you could ask a direct question, such as, 'Do you know anybody that is always complaining about their weight?' You are fishing for any paid-up member of the Chubby Chums Club (BMI >45, terms and conditions apply).

ASSOCIATE: So, what do you think of the opportunity?

PROSPECT: I'm not interested in your weight loss product, thanks.

ASSOCIATE: That's a shame. Any pals in the Chubby Chums Club?

PROSPECT: Never heard of that one.

ASSOCIATE: Any workmates with the BMI of a Stone Troll?

PROSPECT: Nope.

ASSOCIATE: Neighbours called Lard-Arse, Tubby-Tits, Fatberg, Buffalo-Butt?

PROSPECT: None that come to mind. I think I'd know.

ASSOCIATE: Christ, work with me here! Anyone, absolutely anyone with a sarcastic name such as Skinny or Pipe-cleaner or Rear-of-the-Year. Please, think, I have to eat my overhead here!

PROSPECT (Punching a speed dial number in her phone) Hello? Samaritans. Will to Live department, please. Yes, I'll wait, but do hurry.

Let's suspend our disbelief and imagine that a prospect handed over the contact details of a weight-challenged acquaintance. On which planet would you think it acceptable to send a message to your friend that says, 'We asked your friend, Jemima, for the name of a fat friend, and she nominated you and your spare tyre' (the one that looks like the inner tube for a Massey-Ferguson tractor). Watch as the needle on the Cringe Detector swings wildly off the scale.

But your upline ignores your cringe, convinced that you're spreading the love. Everybody from Minsk to Mumbai simply has to know about the opportunity. Opportunities are gifts, and the more people know about them, the healthier the world's population will be. How would you feel if nobody shared a precious gift with you? Umm... no comment.

The Bad - Money

The following negative topic is money. Money can mean different things to different people. I'm not talking about the millions that you will make today, tomorrow, someday, never. I'm speaking about the false belief that there will be money in the 24 carat, gold-plated, near-divine form of passive income. The kind of money that rolls into your bank account while you sleep.

Interesting MLM fact, number 1,852: Did you know that the top one percent who already earn good money still chase money? Why? Because, as a shark must keep moving or die, you must keep on earning to survive. It's MLM's very own perpetual motion machine.

I never met anyone who had inherited an MLM business, as a legacy, from their parents or relatives. Wouldn't that be an exciting reading of a will?

SOLICITOR (to family): And to my darling daughter, Felicity, I leave my collection of Late Victorian thimbles, my ostrich-feather boa, and the MLM business, worth $80 Million.

Yet they burble on about money incessantly. This is premium grade BS. The only legacy that can get passed from generation to generation is from MLM owners. I have lived a sheltered life (My parents told me that Knutsford didn't exist so that I would stay in at night, and I believed them), but non-compliance has shut down some network marketing companies. Some have gone bankrupt; some rebranded, some merged with other MLM companies. This is an industry in flux. It is nowhere near as stable as they'd have you believe. Aliens could have abducted the MDs of these MLM companies and exiled them to Prison Planet Epsilon Delta for all we knew. The fate of MLM companies was yet another taboo subject.

And without living proof of these riches ready to be plucked from the air, I refused to take their word for it. Yeah, money can be good if you are good, and if you are the teacher's pet, the companies can take everything away from you in a flash. Ask too many probing questions and see how long it is before they shunted you up a siding.

Here's just one horror story by way of illustration: A top leader's account was frozen then closed with immediate effect because she started to ask too many questions, questions the company's owners did not want to be asked. I don't have details, but from what little I knew from spying on her Facebook, I sympathised with her family's plight. Their income stopped entirely in a day.

Yet niggling doubts remained. Was her story believable? During her rants about the incident, she posted on social media about how she needed to use discount vouchers for grocery shopping to get by. Coachman, stay the horses! Tell me, how do you slide, in a week, from millionaire status to having to use a 10p off voucher to buy a tin of Bulgarian peas already plastered with 50% off stickers?

The type of money that mattered most to me was the kind you spent on your products to remain active whilst earning diddly squat and running up expenses on par with the national debt of Peru. The situation worsened if your spouse was a customer too because they needed to reorder to stay active.

That's two orders coming out of your credit card balance every month. And if you can't afford to repay the balance at the end of the month, your debt piles up like horse poop in a stable yard until you can barely see over the top of it.

As debts mount, you need to keep tabs on when that 0% interest offer you somehow imagined would last forever comes to a crashing end, forcing you to hunt down the next best 0% credit card deal. I have only just cleared my credit card debt six months after I quit. But I am lucky because I had a steady income that enabled me to repay the debt.

The Bad - Product cost increases

As if you were not already struggling enough, scrambling together the cash to finance your monthly order, along comes more badness in the shape of product price increases. Spending ten to fifteen pounds a day on the system was not enough! Now you had to convince your prospects to continue despite the rise.

It was hard-going convincing anybody before the price went up; now it's a tad more problematic. Best advice from your leaders? Don't say, 'That's too expensive!' Instead, say, 'My health is just not worth the investment' and see how that sounds. Typical guilt-laden advice.

Cringe

The Bad - Bragging

Are you aware that only your network marketing friends brag on social media about how much they earn? They spam you with photographs of your orgasmically happy teammates faces, complete with graphic tabs that advertise their earnings for the week.

I can't speak for others, but for my part, I felt neither jealous nor inspired. Instead, I cringed. By this time, my cringing muscles threatened to cramp through overuse.

They bragged about how many people they managed to dupe into buying their products, and now they waved their bonuses in their customers' faces. Very undignified. For one thing, new customers befriended through their social media would see these posts in glowing technicolour. And they'd realise that the rep's spiel—that it's all about their health and nothing else was pure guano.

The bad - Tax

Let's take stock. You're running your own home business, being your own boss. You don't work for your MLM company—they are your partners. How much support do you think your upline gives you in terms of business setup? For the mathematically minded, the actual figure is nine-tenths of bugger all, or, in layman's terms, zero. Yes, you heard it here first—zero.

They will happily commend you for eating your overhead, and pointing out that your stationery and merchandise are tax-deductible. They'll share the top-secret hack (known to all and sundry) about making sure you keep photos as proof of your home parties. They'll share the figures for hiring market stalls. This you may have willingly. What they won't tell you is how to deal with the rest of your tax affairs. They just like to make it sound attractive that almost everything you do can be written off. Luckily, since I already had a Limited company, I included MLM under the same umbrella, and the little I earned was paid into my corporate account.

I know that my upline isn't a tax advisor and that we are all responsible for our own companies, but what annoyed me most is that they never shared what they did. And the answer to that's revealing—they hadn't a clue how to comply with the regulations that governed their enterprises and thought it best not to encourage HMRC to lend their assistance in the matter. How many reps file accurate tax returns, I wonder? How many angels can you fit on the head of a pin?

As I filed corporate accounts showing losses, I had no tax to pay each year, but I was lucky because I understood the difference between a sole trader and a Limited company. Sadly, your MLM corporation won't support you either, so you are as alone as Jane was before she met Tarzan.

Chapter 19

BEAUTY IS ONLY SKIN DEEP, BUT UGLINESS GOES RIGHT THROUGH TO THE BONE.

In which: Ex-millionaire leaders are publicly slandered — Peggy surpasses the moral standards of Vlad the Impaler and counts that as a win —

What follows, though uglier than the Ugly Duckling after the oak tree fell on her (No, that's a different ugly duckling from another story), is based on observations of high-profile leaders I followed on social media. I was not personally involved.

What I discovered about the dark underbelly of MLM made me glad to be a mere pinprick of light in their stellar organisation, shining so dimly, hardly anyone would notice me. Let the millionaires blaze brightly; I'm happy where I am, thanks.

I want to discuss the uglier side of the business because, initially, I had no idea there even was an ugly side—that some of the things I learned could happen in a family-run MLM business.

It's unsettling—disturbing even—to realise that however respectful a relationship you've had with company owners or other leaders, despite your service, when you jump ship, they disown you. They treat you in the same way Superman treated Lex Luther and cyber-bully you in the most horrendous way. Not only do they cut any ties with you immediately and stop any pay going your way, but they will also do anything in their power to ruin you financially. They bring lawsuits against you, insult you and even drag your children into it if that's what it takes to lay you low.

This is about publicly slandering ex millionaire-leaders. People who travelled the world to speak at events in front of thousands of associates, sacrificing their time and families to mentor strangers. Eek! It was painful to watch!

A story came to me when I started to detach myself from the company and slowly shut down my accounts, removing myself from all the groups and the MLM trap. The horror of this story sealed my belief that I was right to grab my parachute and jump out of the MLM aeroplane before it went into a tailspin.

I can impart the good news early: All leaders featured in this section found themselves new jobs in other MLM companies. They had skills, believed in the business model, and knew they could replicate their former success with their new partners.

Like Katherine, these people could sell ice cubes from a stall in the Arctic Circle. They have a system. They aren't bitter about the MLM business model or feel like failures (unlike me, who quit for good); they just wanted to move on to a different company. It wasn't complicated; they lost faith in the organisation or products. Nothing wrong with that, right?

In a mainstream workplace, people regularly change jobs and companies. Nobody bullies you for finding a new job. You work out your notice and leave. Ex colleagues wish you well; someone will buy a half-bottle of Asti Spumante from the discount section of Bargain Booze and cobble together a makeshift celebration. Afterwards, you remain friends and write endorsements for each other on LinkedIn.

Are you familiar with that picture? Yes? Well, forget about that world altogether. Hear this: There'll be no flowers on your last day with your MLM company. No one will congratulate you on your career change. To them, you died the moment you resigned.

For minions like me, the situation is quite different. You could vanish in a plume of smoke one morning, and nobody would mention your name again. My departure failed to register the Volcanic Explosivity Index (VEI) of 6. The eruption of Krakatoa reported back in the day (equivalent under SI ratings to one billion times as loud as an elephant fart). But then, I had no team to unsettle during my exit or take to a competitor—which is their greatest fear.

The best-laid plans of mice and men, they say, often land tits-up (with apologies to Rabbie Burns), but the company, unfortunately, picked on the wrong people. These leaders were no limp-wristed thumb-sucking namby-pambies who'd go running home to mummy because someone stuck their tongue out at them. Oh no.

These leaders had resilience in depth. They'd let no one kick sand in their face. No whispering behind hands for them. They shouted about their shameful mistreatment from the rooftops to the public (or MLM muggles as they were known) through a megaphone.

While the owners of this particular MLM company contemplated the law of unintended consequences, more and more employees sided with their former leaders, they left to join the new company too. As a mark of the leaders' integrity, they didn't set out to lure existing staff away, but they eventually retaliated when pushed once too often.

It wasn't unknown for leaders with the ethical standards of Vlad the Impaler to extract whole teams to their next MLM company because the prize was great: instant promotion.

Chapter 20

THE RISE AND FALL (AND ABSOLUTE COLLAPSE) OF THE MLM WANNABE MILLIONAIRE.

In which: Peggy mulls over broken hopes and dreams — Continues to sip store-bought cider — Peggy realizes that she knows more about quantum mechanics than MLM marketing, that the world is not her octopus, after all, that network marketing is eternal marketing; like breathing, the minute you stop you die — Peggy reluctantly acknowledges that MLM is not for her.

Broken Dreams Recap

Time to recap on the broken hopes and dreams. What went wrong? Why am I not sitting on a yacht off the British Virgin Islands? Why am I sipping store-bought cider instead of imported French Champagne? Why—and this is the $64,000 question— was no one ever able to show me the money they promised I'd make in my sleep? I mean, I wouldn't have noticed an influx of dosh while I slept, but it should have been tucked up in my current account when I woke up in the morning. It wasn't.

I was in two minds. Part of me thought that MLM generated more misinformation than the Cold War, especially during recruitment. Early expectations could so quickly be dashed. Sometimes, the vendor appeared to be a dream come true, at least at the RFP (request for proposal) stage. With a complete understanding of our joint objectives and a fair wind, the world was our octopus.

If only that loveliness could continue. But it's like getting a puppy. That joyous bundle of fluff—perhaps you've called her Princess Floribundum of Utrecht, a beautiful name—enters your home and your heart, spreading more warmth through your household than your wood-burning stove.

Puppy-hood is but a fleeting phase in a canine's life, though. Within a year, Princess Floribundum of Utrecht will have chewed the legs clean off your Chippendale sideboard and scratched so much of your furniture, your home will have come to resemble the site of a particularly vindictive badger attack. Your 'Princess' always was a wolf. You just didn't know it.

My point is that your dream vendor is like a puppy in that initial, fluffy honeymoon period. It's only once the contracts are signed and the work starts that the wolf comes out of the forest to howl at you.

Words, phrases, clauses, whole pages even start to sound ambiguous. Worse, the vendor may become suspicious of the contract as a whole. At this point—mark these words—your vendor has started chewing the legs off your furniture (editor note: not sure that's right, please check.) To avoid the legal quicksand this entails, I worked hard to pre-empt all ambiguous quotes, statements and promises. But this was just another thing that ate up my time.

However, I wouldn't characterize MLM as good or bad. Depending on how you looked at it, it was both. On the positive side, you could argue that I'd come to MLM by pure chance. I didn't seek to become a rep, nor did I feel that my lifestyle was so rubbish that I had to research what could improve my diet. I just wanted to earn extra money to fund my absolute dream (I read somewhere that God lets you have ten dreams in a lifetime, but which God, I'm not sure—Bassett, perhaps, the God of Liquorice Allsorts?)

I didn't have a Scooby what network marketing entailed. Back then, I didn't even know about the two camps. The die-hard MLM enthusiasts and the die-hard MLM haters. After two year's of complete immersion in MLM, I somehow find myself at home in neither camp. Had I known more (before you jump in at the deep end, due diligence my friends!), I would never have signed up. But I firmly believe we should live our lives without regret. Instead, look back and appreciate the valuable lessons learnt—always there if you look hard enough. For starters, I counted myself lucky to land with a half-decent MLM, yes I came out defeated, and yes I was out of pocket, but I will remain forever grateful for incurring no financial debt I could not afford to repay.

One thing you can be sure of: No one whose purpose in life is to recruit you to MLM will answer your questions frankly. You bet they'll have answers for everything, but their responses will be as vague as a politician's promise. And every single word will have been scripted.

You know that feeling when you suddenly wonder if you dreamed something or it happened? Of course, if you have a memory of being pursued across the Yorkshire Dales by the Dalai Lama on a space hopper, it's a safe bet that was a dream. But in considering whether I had misinterpreted the messages my company sent me, the conclusion was less clear cut.

Had they intentionally taught me to sound as vague as one of Nostradamus's predictions when attempting to talk prospects into signing up? Remember my 3-way call? I remained unclear on what exactly they wanted me to do. Or consume, even.

At some point, you become aware that someone (the Dalai Lama on a space hopper?) is asking for credit card details while you appear to be in an information overload induced trance. By the way, this is a criticism I could aim at all MLM companies, not just the one I worked for.

I recently got a message from a 'friend'. 'Hi hun,' she said. 'I am contacting a few special people in this time of Covid to say I have found the Holy Grail of MLM companies. We can make money hand over fist online, from home via our mobiles without selling! I'm telling only especially special people, and straight away I thought of you. Not sure if you're looking for something right now. If you are, let me know, I can send you a short 19-minute video to give you a better understanding of this wonderful opportunity.'

Here you go. Different company, same hogwash. Not quite telling you what this particular Holy Grail looks like, but 'watch my short 19-minute video, and I will reveal all.' Isn't that exciting! No, it bloody well isn't. It's annoying! And by the way, for the avoidance of doubt, 5 minutes is the internationally recognized duration of *short*. In an era when Lidls will sell you a twelve-course microwaveable Indian meal ready for consumption in under ten minutes, nineteen minutes, for practical purposes, might as well last forever.

I was unworthy. What a privilege that they'd thought to share their news with little old me! How special should I feel? Not very. Because the exact copied and pasted message will have gone to every single person in her contact list!

You see, had the naïve me received this message two years ago; I would most likely have said yes to the video. I'd have watched it, felt compelled to get on a call with her to clarify the details of the introductory, super-vague opportunity. To harvest the hopes and dreams of the laptop lifestyle with its promise of passive income and, who knows, this book would probably turn out precisely the same as it's shaping up now—I would throw in the towel, skint and frustrated, failing to get *my business* off the ground.

To finish the story, I politely asked what she was promoting because I did not want to watch a nineteen-minute video, and she said, 'Why don't you join our group Zoom meeting tonight?'

I tried a more direct approach. 'I'm just nosey,' I said, 'I'd rather marry a walrus than do MLM again.' And voila! She just came out with it. And guess what? She thanked me for my time and asked if I knew anybody who wanted to earn more money. Bravo for sticking with the script and sealing my belief that no matter what MLM you are introduced to; it is not for me.

Do you get paid for eternity?

What do I make of the fundamental MLM assertion, 'Do the work once and get income until the heat death of the universe'? A misunderstanding on my part, or a deliberately misleading quote?

Discounting spouses, it's a safe bet that the number of associates with a still-active first signing can be counted on the fingers of one foot. You can play *Once-Upon-A-Time*, of course. They worked for me once upon a time, I trained them once upon a time and so on. And you can say you are still raking in points from their re-orders. But to benefit from those orders, you must have another die-hard customer or a rep who re-orders from the other side of the tree, with the religious fervour of a Buddhist monk. Otherwise, the points do not convert to money.

Network marketing is never-stop networking; you stop, the money stops. Passive income happens at the top, not to you. Maybe you'll get that yacht in the British Virgin Islands, but you'll never have time to put to sea in it. You'll be too busy looking after the people you introduced to the company. Some of these were high maintenance with daily touchpoints. And I had 25 at most! What must a down-line of 10,000 be like? What do they do with all the queries from needy customers and desperately demotivated consultants?

Don't quit the day job!

Whatever happens, never, ever quit your job! This is a side-hustle to most, an additional stream of income. Unless you are 100% committed and sure that you like this profession and want to become a professional network marketer, only quit your day job when you exceed your monthly income for a few months. And beyond that, feel stable and comfortable enough in your capability to continue to bring the bacon home. Perhaps you have been introduced to MLM during maternity or unemployment. If so, I would still urge you to find a steady job, I know 9-5 isn't everybody's dream—quite the opposite, but it pays the bills.

Please don't delude yourself into thinking you will hit the top 1% simply because they allow you to dream that financial freedom comes through inducing two people to drink protein shakes. We all know two people, and they will know two people (Big dogs have little fleas that sit on them and bite 'em. Little fleas have littler fleas, and so ad infinitum.) Get a grip!

Due diligence

Do your due diligence. Find out how many companies sell protein shakes or whichever products the MLM you are interested in offers. There are more products of a similar nature on the market than a womanizer has excuses. They will tell you that their product beats them all, hands down, and reel off all the benefits and reasons that justify the costs. But it's all rehearsed. There will be no shortage of insiders falling over their Nike Airs to help alleviate whatever ails you. Just bear their vested interest in mind — they'll earn a bonus for signing you up.

I had never had a protein shake in my 40 years of life until my first day on the product. (To be honest, I thought protein shakes were for bodybuilders, and in my youth, they used to drink raw eggs. Yuck!) The change to my usual routine seemed positive. It was convenient, and yeah, I found it tasty.

I lost 20lb in 90 days. I felt good, but I was dependent on powdered food 80% of the time! I had to take my food with me everywhere, including on holiday, to continue this healthy lifestyle. It is all exciting when your mind is in the right place if you are motivated, focused and seeing results. But long term? No, I cannot imagine this being sustainable.

As with any diet based on an abnormal lifestyle, weight maintenance became a struggle. Six months into drinking two shakes a day, my skin became irritated (was somebody sneaking into my room at night to sandpaper my knees?), I constantly felt bloated, as if I just drank eight pints of Guinness.

I switched to the dairy-free shakes that had just come onto the UK market. This resulted from an MLM propaganda onslaught showcasing the purity of whey products from grass-fed cows (three cheers for our bovine brothers!) I somehow managed to *overlook* the fact that I was consuming tons of dairy products, which I had cast out into the nutritional wilderness about 15 years ago. What. A. Total. Douche. Bag! (This was the point that I swapped intro tunes— from It's My Life to *Poison* by Alice Cooper.)

If we're lining up to take the blame, there's only one person in the queue— yours truly.

The dairy-free shakes tasted like blackboard chalk. The vanilla was super grainy and sweeter than treacle. The dairy version was much nicer and was my all-time favourite.

Eighteen months I lasted. A die-hard, protein-shake consumer twice a day, taking all the daily and nightly supplements to support my digestion, and I must say, my body felt as if it was rewarded with a new, top of the range digestive system.

After eighteen months, I have gone down to just one breakfast shake because I discovered—God bless human biology— that I became bloated on the dairy-free shakes too. However, I was no longer clogging my body with the evils of dairy (As an aside, this was the title of a 1971 Hammer House of Horror movie, The Evils of Dairy, starring Peter Cushing in which a bunch of cows terrorize a local mall.)

Gradually, I reduced my consumption to a minimum, perhaps after a good workout in the gym, but that was only to finish all the supplies I had accumulated from all my autoship orders. I have never stopped taking supplements, though, and since my body's digestive system is still working like clockwork, I know I do not need the whole system they lead you to believe you do!

Are MLM products rubbish?

There is a rumour that MLM products are bad. I can't agree with that. You are sure to find some good products if you are selling MLM products; there are so many to choose from. Parting with your company doesn't mean you cannot continue to use their products. You can switch to a customer account instead of the business account and order what you like if your budget allows it.

That's what I do. Well, at least until I can find a genuine replacement for what I benefit from now. The problem remains that the ingredients list reads like the periodic table of the elephants (Editor: Please check the terminology). Finding a similar product is more challenging than scaling the north face of the Eiger with your climbing boots on the wrong feet if you have no idea what's in the one you're using to start with!

I regained all the weight I lost and maintained during my die-hard 18 months on the products. This shows that this is a diet and not a sustainable lifestyle as they like to advertise it. I have never been obese anyway; I just wasn't happy with my figure. I would like to be a smidgen closer to the Gigi Hadid end of the scale, to be honest.

I have a BMI of 23, which is still in the green, healthy range; I just don't fit into size eight jeans any more (Well, I could—with help from a couple of fit friends, but I'd probably need to call the Fire Brigade to cut me out of them. Who could be bothered with that carry on after a night out?)

You would think that a solution that once worked would be worth revisiting. Not so. Throwing yourself off the Clifton Suspension Bridge with a bungee rope around your ankles would be a thrill once, but you wouldn't do it every day, I suspect.

Once I'd lost faith in the products and the company, there was nothing I could do to recover. You must be a serial MLM professional to want to embark on the same journey with another company.

Unshakable Belief in MLM

Where did I go wrong? Why did I fail? Did I do too much or too little? I've gone over everything I've done, all the tools I had available to me, all the advice, forums, zoom calls. I was as forensic as the Silent Witness team. Are these companies and compensation plans designed to make the majority fail? Hence 99% of reps never make it?

Maybe. But I feel I failed because I lacked unshakeable belief in network marketing. I had objections I could not get past. If I can't get rid of my objections, how the heck do I eradicate the prospects' objections? I had no chance!

When somebody said the system was expensive, I agreed with them. When they said the plan left them hungry enough to eat a buffalo between two mattresses (hold the mayo!), I agreed with them. When they said the shakes (some of them) tasted like wallpaper paste, I agreed with them. I can lie, but my face can't! I would sympathize but would not patronize them with idiotic answers like,

'Your health is worth it.'

'You are investing in your health.'

'You'll adjust to the taste; your palate will change the healthier you become.'

I failed, too, because other people knew more about network marketing than I did. It felt like every day was my first day at work, but everyone else was a seasoned pro. I had no business experience first-hand, nor had I been lured into MLM in my adult life. From all the previous occasions I talked about earlier, like Avon and Kleeneze, I learned that nobody ever wanted to compete in their region, so they never recruited. They wanted to be the only rep in the village, so they got all the business.

I was adequately naïve when I started, told to be grateful I had been introduced to the most ethical and generous MLM company on the planet as my first company (Sing three loud Hosannas and bang that tambourine). Some people have to go through several crap companies before finding their spiritual MLM 'home', don't you know? I was without a frame of reference. I knew nothing. I believed them. On reflection, I feel like a proper tool. But that's life. And that is why I fell victim.

Other than my lack of faith, ignorance of the MLM sector, and naïvety, the fourth reason for failure loomed large—I could never bring myself to do anything to which I morally objected. No matter how many times they urged me to step outside my comfort zone, I couldn't do it. I would have needed to take anti-cringe medication, and there never seemed to be enough of that to hand.

To put this more accurately, I couldn't do it now. Once maybe I might have given it my best shot, swallowed down my awkwardness and just gone for it. But do that repeatedly? No way. My upline had an answer for this, as she had an answer for everything in MLM—I was uncoachable. From my point of view, I called it being somebody's puppet. So what if I missed out on the big bucks because of my uncoachable nature. I can at least live with myself and sleep at nights.

I failed, I don't care; and I'm not bitter; I underwent two years of personal development training, understanding people's behaviour, learning about nutrition, making new friends, discovering worlds I never knew existed.

It's simple. Network marketing is not for me. Never was, never will be. Fool me once, they say, shame on you, fool me twice, shame on me. There isn't going to be a second time for me, however hard the MLM devil may tempt me. Admittedly, it's not much of a motivational slogan, but it happens to be true: I was rubbish before, and I will be rubbish again.

If you are sitting with a fence post up your butt, undecided whether to cut the chains and leave MLM for good, consider this: if you've not ranked in the first 90 days, the likelihood is that your conscious and unconscious objections have conspired to hole the good ship Fame & Fortune below the waterline. Then, no matter how many events you go to or how many zoom calls you attend with millionaire mentors, I'm sorry to break it to you, but your chances of success are thinner than the ham in a Salvation Army sandwich.

Cut your losses and go. Sling your hook. You can send me a postcard from a better place when you get there. Hanging around waiting for the gravy train to pull up at platform three, you'll only get disappointed. Had you been 100% committed, you would have found a way by now. And in this game, if 99% is all you can muster, I'd advise you to pack up your tent and jog on.

Think about it. Those wanting to become lawyers or airline pilots put 100% of their efforts into becoming one. They did not procrastinate; they focused all their energy on that 'one thing' to achieve their ultimate goal. Those that couldn't cut it quit. That is why they never became lawyers or pilots. Duh! They moved on to find something else. Being a doctor or a pilot is a zero-sum game. You are either a pilot or not. Similarly, you can't be half a doctor. Otherwise, you'd get this:

RECEPTIONIST: The doctor will see you now, madam. He's allowed to hold a stethoscope to your chest, but he's not yet qualified to listen.

PATIENT: That's okay; I feel half better already!

I can just imagine all the intransigent MLM folks scowling at me right now, over the top of their sanctimonious spectacles, even though I don't see any of them ever reading this book. They'd say that expecting any MLM business to be an overnight success would be like planting a single acorn on a Monday and hoping to find a forest of mighty oak by the weekend.

You need long-term thinking. You should be asking, *where would you like to be in five years?* This is yet another fallacy, however. With the possible exception of my uncle Toby (don't ask), nobody is dumb enough to think they will be a millionaire after 90 days. It would be pretty spectacular to reach these dizzy heights in five years. But to get anywhere near a regular, seven-figure income, you'd need divine intervention. The odds of this are the same as a hurricane blowing through a scrap yard and randomly assembling an 80-foot high statue of Engelbert Humperdinck.

You do the maths. An associate earning forty quid a week every three to four weeks will have a 5-year forecast gloomier than a wet weekend in Manchester.

Here is a little tip for those that believe in MLM but find their company old-fashioned, their customer acquisition methods outdated. There is a better way. Have you heard the buzz phrase 'social marketer'? No? It's the future of MLM. Apparently. Google it. I am through with network marketing.

Good afternoon folks. Today we will be flying at a height of 200 feet 17 and one half inches. We should be flying at 34,000 feet, but Bob, your pilot for today isn't allowed above 200 feet until he finishes his training. Keep an eye out for mobile phone masts, because Bob hasn't had the results of his eye test back yet either

Do I have regrets?

I remain ever the optimist, despite my accelerating plunge through MLM. It's a descent that felt uncannily like hurtling down a bobsled run with my butt perched precariously on one of those tea-trays bobsledders travel on—a luge I think it's called.

You'd think I'd be cursing the clairvoyant who introduced me to MLM. After all, I wasted two years of my life doing something I'm not good at and got myself into debt. And in the end, the only thing I succeeded in was pushing myself further away from my original dream of having my private label product by failing to earn the capital I needed to get started.

I don't see it that way. I have no hard feelings. I am grateful to her because the last two years have proved to be a valuable experience that I had to undergo to discover myself.

I was exposed to a world I had never experienced before nor knew existed. I embarked on a journey of self-development. Yes, I made sacrifices. I spent more money than I would ever have done on groceries. I could have lived off Fortnum and Mason luxury hampers and paid less.

When I say I learnt about nutrition, it doesn't mean I agreed with drinking protein meal replacements. I became curious about what the body needs on the micro-level, protein pasting, and the various supplements necessary for my body to tick. I educated myself about such things during this process.

I had a reasonably healthy lifestyle before joining my company, but most of my food intake comprised carbohydrates, fruit and veg. I shunned protein, red meat in particular, because my body simply said, 'Sorry mate, but I can't handle this.'

This was the beautiful thing about the whole system: my body worked like clockwork, I was able to eat what I wanted without struggling the following day. First, I thought that it was the shakes and the combination of all the products I consumed daily, but I came to realize that it was the supplements that helped my body function, so that's why I'm sticking with them until I find replacements.

And if I don't find replacements, I'll just get my supplies from my former MLM company. I like many of the energy and performance products too, but using my common-sense, non-MLM-brainwashed hat, they are bloody expensive, and I'm sure I'll easily find replacements on the market. Gone are the days when you had to trek cross-country in hiking gear to the Holland & Barrett shop in the next village but one, in search of soluble vitamin C. Nowadays, supermarkets and Amazon have dietary supplements in abundance.

I don't regret leaving MLM when I did.

I fought an ongoing battle between my head and soul. I did the vision boards, read all the recommended self-development books, watched all the vimeos, surrounded myself with positivity, made the lists, a 90-day plan, studied all the successful folks, and tried to follow the system. I wanted to be an expert. I was determined to succeed. But I did not have what it takes.

I was not prepared to do everything they told me to do. I almost wish I'd quit earlier because I now realize that you will never have a successful MLM business as long as you have objections, reservations, or doubts. And are, in their eyes, uncoachable.

Whatever possessed me to conclude after each event, after I was all pumped up like a ninja warrior, that I'd take massive action as if my life depended on it? Who knows—brainwashing, maybe?

After I decided to stop this madness, I embarked on a digital rampage to delete shake posts from my social media. I also removed educational posts related to the MLM products and people I didn't want to be friends with in the first place but felt obliged to back in the day. I removed myself from every MLM group, unfollowed all the leaders I stalked, changed my social media bio, updated my LinkedIn profile intro and removed myself from every messenger and WhatsApp group.

I felt cleansed! Finally free. The relief - like the only coffee I could afford to buy during those two years— was instant. No more dreaded notifications I had to read immediately. I was free! I was able to leave my phone unattended without being crippled by guilt. Boy, did I feel good!

The only thing that bothers me is all those un-read LinkedIn introduction messages, where I was trying to connect with fresh blood and entice people to look at 'my opportunity'. *Awkward!* I no longer had an opportunity, so I hope they remain un-read or un-responded to.

And I feel a pinch of guilt that my children looked up to me, yet I made them believe that a liquid diet is the only healthy way to live your life. Luckily neither of them have been scarred for life (though nobody yet knows the long term effects on the developing mind of watching In the Night Garden starring Iggle Piggle and Makka Pakka.) They enjoy a variety of foods too. Some people make good money from MLM. Not all MLM organizations run scams. Yet the truth is that the MLM business model isn't everybody's mug of Darjeeling.

You may fail at network marketing, but all is not lost so long as you realize it isn't how you want to earn a living. Compose yourself. 'Failure is the seed of growth.' There, I've said it. Gather your thoughts and learning. Pat yourself on the back for giving it a shot (you can pat yourself on the front if you prefer, but it'll look odd.)

Frame this as one more experience under your belt. Just like the jobs you have had in the past that did not float your catamaran! You did not fail at them; you quit them. I once left a job in a chocolate factory after only three weeks! I genuinely could not stand the sight and smell of all that sugary stuff any longer. No way I intended to stick around in the hope of climbing the ranks and becoming the next chocolate factory CEO.

Use all the positivity and personal development you learned to power something useful. All skills are transferable, and you never know when they'll come in handy!

EPILOGUE

Having painstakingly arranged more than 60,000 words into twenty concise chapters, perhaps a final summary of this book's key messages might prove helpful to anyone considering MLM as a career.

Below, I list what I consider to be the top five must-have qualities for success in MLM. Used as a scorecard and counting 10 points per quality, my performance would have equalled the United Kingdom's 2021 Eurovision Song Contest score of 'Null Points,' which shows how miserable a failure I proved to be in the industry.

Whatever you do, don't let my failure dissuade you from chasing your entrepreneurial dreams. In the two years I took to trip over my shoelaces and fall flat on my face in the MLM business, many succeeded — some spectacularly so.

Peggy's Five Must-Have Qualities for MLM Success

1. You'll need to love selling more than Juliet loved Romeo.

Selling is the premier way to progress in any job featuring a product or a service. This is especially true of MLM. A battle-hardened MLM saleswoman, as excited about her next sale as a hippopotamus anticipating a mud bath, is beyond doubt, bound for glory.

Such born and bred salespeople could sell out Wembley Arena hosting a Covid-restricted socially-distanced boxing match. But they could just as soon sell whelks by the pound from a stall on Blackpool seafront — because selling's in their DNA.

It follows, then, that if you'd rather pull your brains out through your nose with a crotchet hook than take a sales job, shepherding supermarket trolleys back to their pick up point might offer you a brighter future because, without a passion for selling, your MLM dream ship is holed beneath the waterline, and guaranteed to sink.

2. You'll need to understand your chosen language thoroughly

Learn your mother tongue thoroughly. Skip the historical stuff — you'll have no need of a single hey-nonny-nonny, an 'Alas poor Yorick' or even an odds bodkins. It's contemporary usage you want to study to help you understand the precise meanings of the avalanche of words, phrases, jargon and memes MLM will rain down on you from the get-go.

3. You'll need the wisdom to distinguish hard work from productivity

I get that, in English at least, the bumblebee seems wedded to the adjective 'busy.' Though, quite why we should celebrate its busy nature always baffled me. Because, outside of the beehive, we humans need to ditch 'busy' for 'productive.' Busy won't get results; productive will. Given a choice between working hard and working smart, opt for smart any day.

4. You'll need to know the business like the back of both hands.

As a rule of thumb, whatever business you've set your mind on, make sure you know as much about it as you can. Get up close and kick the tires before climbing into the driving seat. This counts double for MLM because, in MLM, ignorance is seldom bliss. The whole learn-while-you-earn shtick perpetrated by the MLM industry is pure, unadulterated horse manure. The notion that you should just throw yourself in at the deep end and thrash around until somehow you magically learn how to swim is barely credible.

Besides, show me anyone willing to hand over a roll of tenners fit to choke a mule to an uninspiring MLM newbie winging her way through her early career with reckless abandon, and I'll show you gormless Jack (of beanstalk fame) trading his mother's only cow (forward slash, last remaining asset) for a handful of magic beans.

5. You'll need to be a 'people' person.

The world and his wife will tell you that a business's greatest asset is its people. This is undoubtedly true of MLM. So, suppose you are a professional wallflower, Shrinking Violet's more bashful sister, Cowering Katie, or just someone who prefers the company of cockapoos to people. In that case, I recommend you try your hand at a more solitary pursuit, such as navel-gazing or playing patience.

*

You could build the foundation of a brand new career on my five qualities — and still, fail! Then again, you could ignore them all and end up retiring at 40 to your own Caribbean island. I never intended to offer hard and fast rules, just guidance based on my experience. Whichever path you opt for, I wish you luck and good fortune.

www.ingramcontent.com/pod-product-compliance
Lightning Source LLC
Chambersburg PA
CBHW051112050726
47592CB00002B/789

* 9 7 8 1 9 1 9 6 0 7 3 0 6 *